DIARA KENDRICH

The Inner-First Leader

A 30-Day Practice for Transforming How You Lead From the Inside Out

This book is dedicated to Skylar and Carter, who teach me daily about presence, patience, and purpose, and to my husband, whose partnership grounds and strengthens my leadership.

It is also dedicated to the leaders and mentors who modeled integrity, courage, and growth, and whose guidance continues to shape my path.

Leading yourself well fills your cup.
Compassion keeps it full – so it can be poured
into the lives of many.

~ Diara Kendrich

Contents

III   Part III: Leading Outward

Introduction

What if this season of leadership isn't about doing more, but about becoming more aware?

This book is designed to be experienced - not rushed.

It is a 30-day practice meant to meet you where you are and walk with you, one day at a time. Each chapter represents a daily focus - an invitation to pause, reflect, and lead with greater intention from the inside out.

You are not expected to master anything in thirty days. This is not about perfection or performance. It's about awareness, alignment, and consistency. Some days will feel affirming. Others may stretch you. Both are necessary parts of growth.

Throughout this journey, I share personal and professional lived experiences - stories from my own leadership path, moments of growth, challenge, and learning. These reflections are not meant to position me as an expert who has it all figured out, but as a fellow traveler who understands that leadership is shaped through real experiences, not theory alone.

The first part of this journey begins inward. You'll explore the foundations that shape who you are as a leader - your vision, values, confidence, resilience, energy, and courage. Before leadership is visible, it is internal. These chapters invite you to slow down and reconnect with what anchors you.

The second part moves into practice. Leadership is not just who we are, but how we show up daily. Through discipline, boundaries, emotional intelligence, authenticity, purpose, gratitude, adaptability, influence, relationships, and legacy, you'll examine the habits, choices, and patterns that influence your leadership over time.

The final part turns outward. Leadership ultimately extends beyond self. You'll reflect on service, mentorship, advocacy, collaboration, visionary leadership, integrity, innovation, empowerment, and balance - how your inner work impacts others and how you sustain yourself along the way.

You can move through this book one chapter per day or at a pace that fits your life. You may choose to journal, sit quietly with the reflections, or revisit certain chapters more than once. Trust what you need in each moment.

This is a practice, not a checklist.

The goal is not to rush through thirty days, but to be present with them. To notice what comes up. To listen. To grow.

Leading from the inside out requires intention. It requires honesty. And it requires the willingness to keep becoming.

Consider this your invitation to begin - one day, one choice, one moment at a time.

I

Part I: Inner Foundations

Leadership begins within. This section invites you to slow down, reflect, and strengthen the internal anchors - your values, beliefs, self-awareness, and purpose - that quietly shape how you show up each day. Before influence reaches others, it must first be rooted in clarity and alignment within yourself.

Day 1: Childhood Reflections

"A bird doesn't sing because it has an answer, it sings because it has a song." ~
Maya Angelou

Words can shape how we see the world and ourselves. From the time I was a little girl, I felt the warmth and weight of words. I grew up as an only child for the first nine years of my life, in a single-parent home. Although my mother raised me, my father was very present in my life. I spent many weekends and summers with him, and he never missed an award ceremony or theatrical performance. He was, and still is, deeply invested in my intellectual growth. On top of that, my extended family was deeply loving — maternal and paternal grandparents, aunts, uncles, cousins, and the neighborhood aunties.

My mother and I witnessed harsh realities where we lived — violence, drugs, and few resources. Still, we had each other. We had joy and laughter. We had a kind of wealth that money couldn't buy: love, protection, and community.

I evolved to become someone who cared deeply for others, especially those who had even less than I did. Empathy was nurtured in me at an early age as I watched people survive and still smile through distressing circumstances. I was a straight-A student, cheered on by my teachers who saw my potential and poured into me with their words and support. Their encouragement made me feel seen and capable. I became a leader — not because I had everything, but because I was rooted in love and possibility.

At age nine, my world expanded as I became the eldest of four siblings. That brought new responsibility, but also deepened my understanding of leadership through nurturing and example. I developed strong friendships, some of which I still maintain today. And while I embraced my inner circle and those I loved dearly, I remember the sting of negative words, especially from bullies or people outside of my family who didn't see my light. But even those words shaped me. They made me want more. They made me want to be more.

We may not realize how much our early environment and relationships shape the way we lead ourselves. Childhood plants seeds for how we talk to ourselves, see others, and move through the world. Positive words helped me thrive. Negative words challenged me to grow. All of it mattered. All of it still speaks to me today.

As you begin this journey of leading from the inside out, I invite you to reflect on your own story — not to judge it, but to understand it. Let your self-knowledge be the foundation for authentic leadership and purposeful action.

Self-Reflection Questions

What are some of the earliest words — whether affirming or discouraging — that you remember shaping how you saw yourself as a child?

How did your childhood environment influence the way you lead yourself or respond to challenges today?

Day 2: Power in Self-Talk

"The way you speak to yourself dictates your level of self-love. Speak light. Speak life." ~ Iyanla Vanzant

I carried the words of others like badges for many years - some shiny and affirming, others heavy and hard to shake. Sometimes it was from my parents, family members, friends, or even passing strangers, and their voices all layered onto how I came to see myself. Those words encouraged me, shaped my self-esteem, and helped me believe in myself. Other words chipped away at parts of me I was still getting to know.

By the time I reached my early teens, something inside me clicked. A confidence began to rise - one that whispered. You can do anything you put your mind to. I couldn't wait to grow up. High school felt like freedom on the horizon. College seemed to be the place where independence lived. I imagined moving out of my childhood home, decorating my dorm room, driving my own car, working a real job, and living on my own terms. That version of adulthood seemed exciting - it felt like everything I had worked so hard for would finally make sense.

That confidence carried me through...until it didn't.

I still remember when it shifted. It was middle school, and a new girl had transferred in - popular from the moment she arrived. She was beautiful, stylish, and had what everyone back then called "good hair." People gravitated towards her, especially one of my closest friends. Before I knew it, my friend and this new girl became inseparable - and I suddenly found myself on the outside.

One day, something just changed. My friend turned cold. The new girl followed. Suddenly, every hallway was a battlefield. I was picked apart daily - laughed at for how skinny I was, teased for my "nappy" hair, and called ugly to my face. They found a way to make my existence into a punchline, and for the first time, I started to believe the words. I began to question everything I thought I knew about myself.

It hit deep. It hurt in ways I didn't know how to talk about at the time.

But then one day, my English teacher - someone who had quietly been paying attention - pulled me aside. He looked me in the eyes and said, "Diara, you are brilliant. You're going to do something great with your life. But part of that greatness will involve walking through moments where people won't want to acknowledge it. Instead, they'll try to tear you down. You can't wait for someone to build you back up. You have to build yourself up daily. Speak to yourself with power, with truth. There's strength in the words you tell yourself."

I didn't know it at the time, but that conversation planted a seed that would grow into one of my most important life lessons: the power of self-talk.

I'd heard the phrase before, but this time it stuck. Sometimes it takes walking through pain for a message to resonate finally. We remember truth when we use it to survive - and it works.

There was another moment with that same English teacher I'll never forget. A new guy had transferred to our school, and he was a hit - tall, good-looking, athletic, and the kind of guy everyone noticed. One day during class, he passed me a classic note that read: "Do you like me? Yes or No". My teacher saw the note, smiled, and later pulled me aside. Jokingly, he said, "Diara, your IQ is over 100. His? Maybe a five. Choose wisely."

Now, in today's world, that comment probably wouldn't fly - but back then, it cracked me up. More than anything, it reminded me to value my mind, to hold myself to a standard higher than attention or popularity. And that wisdom stayed with me, even as I moved into high school and beyond.

Over the years, I developed a habit of positive self-talk. I learned to pray, to meditate, and to speak life over myself. I sang affirmations, often. I stood in front of the mirror and reminded myself of who I was and who I was becoming. Especially in challenging seasons, I returned to that inner voice - repeating what I needed to hear until I believed it again.

What we tell ourselves - good, bad, or indifferent - shapes everything. It's not just about confidence. It's about vision. It's about healing. It's about calling yourself back when the world tries to distract, diminish, or detour you.

Self-talk isn't about pretending life isn't hard - it's about strengthening your spirit so you can navigate life with resilience. It's about choosing your words on purpose. Because when you're in the thick of a challenge, and it feels like no one else understands, your voice might be the only one you have. And when that voice is rooted in truth, love, and purpose? You become unstoppable.

This kind of intentional inner dialogue is more than personal growth - it's leadership. When we master the art of speaking power into ourselves, we model something transformative for those around us. It shows up in how we lead our teams, our families, our children, and our communities. We set the tone for what's possible by the way we speak to ourselves when no one's watching.

There's deep power in self-talk. It is not just a coping skill - it's a cornerstone for living and leading well. So today, I challenge you: Pay attention to your inner words. Replace the old lies with new truth. Speak life over yourself, every single day.

Self-Reflection Questions

What are the most common thoughts or phrases you repeat to yourself – and are they building you up or breaking you down?

When you're facing challenges, what would change if you replaced doubt or fear with words of affirmation and truth?

Day 3: The Blueprint of Believing in Yourself

"You become what you believe." ~ Oprah Winfrey

After completion of middle school - a chapter of life that came with its share of challenges, including rejection from close friends and strangers - I made a conscious decision: I would no longer allow negative experiences to define me. Instead, I chose to treat each one as a lesson, an opportunity to grow stronger and wiser. Those lessons became the quiet fuel that carried me into ninth grade with something powerful: a confidence anchored in humility.

It was the kind of confidence that didn't need to be loud, but it gave me the courage to step outside of my comfort zone. I told myself that even if fear showed up, I would show up too. And so, I decided to try new things, explore my interests, and embrace opportunities I once would have thought were "for someone else."

I was a straight-A student, making the super honor roll my first year. But academics weren't the only arena in which I wanted to excel. I joined the school gospel choir and landed a few solos. I auditioned for my very first high school play, Grease, and landed the lead role of Sandy. That meant memorizing lines, singing, and, to my surprise, kissing a popular husky guy in front of a large audience.

I also joined a few student councils, eager to learn the art of collaboration and decision-making. But one of the boldest choices I made was trying out for the cheerleading team.

Now, let me be clear - I had no cheerleading background. I couldn't do a split, a cartwheel, or even a spread-eagled jump. Most of the girls had been cheering since they were little. Me? I had enthusiasm and vision - and that was about it.

When I told my mom about my plan to try out, she asked gently, "Are you sure?"

"Yes," I answered, without hesitation.

I knew the odds weren't in my favor, but I could see myself on that team. I pictured myself at football games, cheering my heart out. I imagined myself along with my teammates in our green and gold uniforms, at competitions, cheering at our homecoming games, and marching proudly in school parades. The image was so clear in my mind that it felt real. And because I could see it, I believed it.

Audition day came and went. Not long after, the phone rang at home. My mom answered, then called me to speak to the unknown caller. It was the cheerleading coach.

Her voice was serious at first, which made my stomach drop. But then she said the words that made me light up: "Congratulations, you've been selected for Junior Varsity."

I was humbled and grateful - JV felt like the perfect starting place. But before I could even process the good news, she added, "Stay tuned...captain auditions are coming up soon."

The word "captain" caught me off guard. For a moment, doubt crept in. Wasn't it already a stretch for me to be on the team at all? But then another thought followed quickly: if I could believe my way into becoming a cheerleader, why couldn't I believe my way into becoming a captain?

So, I decided to go for it.

Similar to the first audition, I prepared physically and mentally, stretching, practicing my jumps, and rehearsing routines to give my best. The captain's audition combined physical skill assessments with a leadership interview. I gave it my best - leading cheers, answering questions about teamwork, and sharing ideas for improving the squad.

When it was over, I felt...okay. Not overly confident, but not defeated either. I decided that even if I didn't get it, I would still walk away proud.

During the waiting period, I practiced stillness - something rare for a high schooler buzzing with anticipation. And in that stillness, I saw another vision: me, wearing that title, leading, encouraging, and creating new routines.

And then the call came.

I had been chosen as captain. Another girl would serve as co-captain, but I was officially the leader of a squad of nine, most of whom had years more experience than I did.

It was the first time in my life that I had led in a space where I was not the most technically skilled. But that didn't matter. My role wasn't just to do the cheers; it was to guide the team, to bring out the best in them, to help us function as one unit. I created new cheers, designed formations, and helped keep morale high through both wins and losses.

And it all happened because I believed in myself.

That experience taught me something I've carried with me through every chapter of my life.

What we tell ourselves, and what we believe, can become our reality.

We have to see it first. Then follow up with intentional action.

Believing isn't just a mindset. It's a skill. And like any skill, it can be developed.

As leaders, we must first believe in our abilities to lead ourselves - to make decisions, take responsibility, and grow from mistakes. Then we must believe in our ability to lead others - to inspire them, challenge them, and help them see possibilities they might not see yet.

Belief is contagious. When a leader truly believes in their vision, their team, and the mission, that belief spreads. It influences change. It encourages others to rise and become leaders in their own right.

Self-Reflection Questions

What's one area of your life where you've held back because you didn't believe you were ready or qualified?

If you saw yourself succeeding in that space - vividly and without limitation - how would that change the actions you take today?

Day 4: Knowing Who You Are

"Success is to be measured not so much by the position that one has reached in life as by the obstacles which he has overcome." ~ Booker T. Washington

I graduated from high school with honors, spent my junior and senior years as a varsity cheerleader, sang solos in the gospel choir, and built friendships that would last a lifetime. But my proudest moment came with the acceptance letter to my dream school - Spelman College. That single envelope represented years of hard work: maintaining a high GPA, transitioning from girlhood to womanhood, and preparing to join a community of intelligent, ambitious women from all walks of life.

Leaving Ohio for Atlanta was both exhilarating and terrifying. I still remember the drop-off vividly - my parents driving away as I stood among hundreds of young women who looked like me. For the first time in my life, I was surrounded by this many women of color in one space. It was overwhelming, but I also felt a deep sense of belonging. I didn't have all the answers about how to live on my own, but I knew I was exactly where I was supposed to be.

The very next day, reality set in. Independence meant making my own decisions, managing my time, and taking responsibility for my future. Thankfully, my two roommates felt the same uncertainty, and that common bond helped us quickly adjust. By the end of the first week, I realized that none of us had it figured out - we were all just learning together.

Initially, I declared computer science as my major, paired with a minor in theater and drama. I chose computer science because it seemed "safe" and promised financial stability after graduation. The arts, on the other hand, fed my soul, so I couldn't let it go completely. But by the end of my first semester, I knew computer science wasn't for me. I wasn't passionate about it. While it was difficult, that decision marked the beginning of an important lesson: finding myself meant being honest about what did and didn't align with who I was becoming.

Unfortunately, that lesson came alongside a significant setback. At the end of my first year, I received notice that my financial aid wouldn't cover sophomore tuition. My parents couldn't make up the difference. I had no choice but to leave Spelman.

I moved back to Ohio, enrolled in community college, and worked retail jobs to pay for classes out of pocket. It was exhausting, but necessary. At 20 years old, I landed an entry-level corporate role as an analyst - my first taste of the professional world. While I never returned to a four-year program right away, I did earn a real estate license to broaden my options. Life was moving quickly: bills, rent, and independence became my reality.

But I always knew I'd return to finish what I started.

Five years into corporate life, a significant issue of workplace discrimination shook me deeply. My leader was eventually suspended, but the experience left me unsettled. I felt stuck - professionally and personally. After much prayer, I made the bold decision to leave Ohio behind and start fresh in Atlanta. I packed only what could fit in my car. It was terrifying, but it was also freeing.

Atlanta became a rebirth for me. I learned that sometimes leading your own life means leaving things behind, even when it's uncomfortable. Less than a year later, I met the man who would become my husband. Seven months into dating, he proposed. Seventeen years, a family, and multiple ventures later, we're still building together. Along the way, I returned to school, completed my bachelor's and master's degrees, advanced in my career, and grew through every trial.

Looking back, I see how every setback prepared me. Being forced to pause my education taught me resilience. Struggling financially sharpened my resourcefulness. Facing discrimination revealed my courage. Each challenge gave me greater clarity about who I was and what I stood for.

That's the heart of this chapter: self-awareness.

Leaders must know who they are — their strengths, weaknesses, values, and triggers. They must also learn how to turn challenges into growth opportunities. I've learned that failure isn't the end; it's a redirection. Every obstacle I've faced has been a mirror, reflecting lessons that improved my self-awareness and shaped me into the leader I am today.

The journey of understanding yourself doesn't come without discomfort. It requires independence, trial and error, setbacks, and faith. But through it all, you "grow through what you go through."

And as a leader, never forget: your worst day might be someone's best day. If you can learn to lead yourself through challenges, you'll be equipped to lead others - through both the easy seasons and the hard ones.

Self-Reflection Questions

When you think about your identity, what words come to mind first? Are these words chosen by you or given to you by others?

How do you define success for yourself - apart from how others may define it for you?

Day 5: When Your Vision Is Clear

"Don't sit down and wait for the opportunities to come. Get up and make them." ~
Madam C.J. Walker

When I look back on my journey, I realize that vision was the anchor that carried me, even when life didn't seem to line up with my dreams. From my early days working in corporate America to relocating to Atlanta, I navigated more dead-end jobs than I can count. Some were to pay the bills, others were stepping stones that didn't lead anywhere meaningful. But through it all, I carried a vision: to one day become a leader in corporate America or to own my own business.

That vision was birthed out of pain. Much of my early experience in the workplace was shaped by bad leadership — the kind that tears people down rather than builds them up. Whether I was the one being mistreated or simply a witness to others being devalued, it left an imprint on me. I saw how poor leadership could distort someone's self-worth, crush their motivation, and even impact their livelihood. It was heartbreaking to watch, and when I personally experienced mistreatment, it left scars. I remember sleepless nights, slipping into moments of depression, and questioning my own value.

But even in the middle of that pain, I made a decision: If I ever had the opportunity to lead, I would not lead like this. I would become the kind of leader who restored, uplifted, and inspired.

My first opportunity came in the car rental business. I started as an agent and was later promoted to manager. At the time, team morale was low, and the workplace environment was draining. But I didn't just accept it as "the way things are." I sat down and wrote out a plan. That plan included daily morning pep talks to motivate the team, creating training opportunities to build skills, sharing best practices from top performers, and coaching on behaviors that didn't align with our goals.

It didn't change overnight, but little by little, things shifted. The team began to show up differently. The atmosphere improved. I saw firsthand that when vision is paired with action, transformation follows. That early leadership experience planted something in me — a deep understanding that vision is not just an idea, it is a tool for change.

From that point forward, I carried my vision into every role I accepted. Eventually, I found myself working in the airline industry, where the scale of leadership expanded beyond anything I had imagined. I led teams ranging from 2 to 160 direct reports. I took on leadership roles in talent development, employee engagement, and diversity, equity, and inclusion. Each step wasn't random — it aligned with the vision I had written in my heart years before.

But vision isn't only about where you're going; it's also about your why. For me, the "why" was rooted in a desire to create healthier, more empowering workplace experiences for people. I knew what it felt like to be diminished by poor leadership, and I refused to replicate that pattern. That clarity drove me to pursue a master's degree in Industrial-Organizational Psychology. I wanted to expand my knowledge in leadership, development, and organizational effectiveness. I wanted not only to lead but also to help transform people and cultures.

The truth is, vision without action is just a dream. But when vision is clear, specific, and paired with intentional steps, it creates a roadmap for your life.

Without vision, it's easy to drift. You can work hard and still go nowhere. You can stay busy and remain stuck. But with vision, your decisions, relationships, and energy all align with your greater purpose. Vision gives you direction when things feel uncertain. It gives you discipline when distractions try to pull you away.

As leaders of ourselves and others, vision is non-negotiable. It is the guiding light that keeps us moving forward even when challenges come. It doesn't just change your life; it transforms the lives of everyone you impact.

3 Actionable Steps to Strengthen Your Vision

1. Write It Down With Clarity: Take time to put your vision on paper. Be specific — don't just say "I want to be successful." What does success look like for you? Where are you working? What kind of leader are you? How are you impacting others? Clarity sharpens focus, and writing it down makes it real.

2. Align Your Decisions With Your Vision: Before saying yes to a new role, opportunity, or even a commitment of your time, pause and ask: Does this align with my vision? Does it move me closer to the life I see for myself? If the answer is no, give yourself permission to say no. Protect your vision with discipline.

3. Review and Refine Regularly: Vision is not static — it grows as you grow. Set aside time, whether quarterly or annually, to review your vision and make adjustments. As you evolve, your vision will expand. Refine it so it continues to challenge and inspire you.

Your vision is the fuel that drives your journey. It is what transforms hardship into purpose and setbacks into stepping stones. Without vision, we live by default; with vision, we live by design. Hold fast to it, nurture it, and take action — because vision, paired with purpose, can change not only your life but the lives of everyone you touch.

Self-Reflection Questions

What is your vision for your life or career?

What is one bold step you can take in the next 30 days to move closer to your vision?

Day 6: Anchoring Your Values

"If I didn't define myself for myself, I would be crunched into other people's fantasies for me and eaten alive." ~ Audre Lorde

Leadership begins with self-reflection. Before we can lead others with confidence, we must know who we are and what we stand for. Anchoring your values is about grounding yourself in that truth - defining what matters most and refusing to let the winds of expectation pull you away from it.

Our values don't form in a vacuum. They are shaped by our lived experiences, our upbringing, our faith, our culture, and the moments that tested us. I know this deeply, as my own values grew from lessons learned in childhood, through family traditions, and the people who modeled compassion and strength. But at some points, we must go beyond what we inherited or absorbed. We must take ownership of what our values mean to us, internally.

Because it's one thing to say, "I value integrity" - and another to define how integrity looks, feels, and shows up in your decisions when no one is watching. It's one thing to say, "I value respect" - and another to hold to that respect even when faced with someone who challenges you or disagrees with your every move. Anchoring your values means you've decided that who you are on the inside will not shift based on the outside.

Values are not just beliefs; they are the anchors that hold you steady when leadership gets hard - and it will get hard. There will be moments when you question your decisions, when doing what's right feels lonely, or when pressure tempts you to compromise. In those moments, your values will either drift or keep you grounded.

Anchored leaders are not perfect. They are consistent. They are guided. They make decisions from a place of alignment rather than from a place of reaction. They understand that leadership isn't about pleasing everyone, it's about staying true to what's right, even when others don't understand.

I can think of so many leaders I've encountered, from my elementary teacher who refused to bend her standards because she cared about our growth, to corporate leaders who stayed steady in the face of politics and pressure. They led from their anchors. Even when others disagreed, the outcome was often favorable, because their actions were rooted in authenticity and fairness, not popularity.

That's the essence of values-based leadership - it's not about doing what's easy, it's about doing what's right. Not because someone's watching, but because you've made a quiet commitment to yourself that this is who you are.

So, what are your core values?

When I reflect on my own, they are simple - yet they run deep.

- To treat others the way I would want to be treated.
- To care for others.
- To lead with integrity.

No matter the setting - personal or professional, in a boardroom or a family room - these principles never fail me. They keep me aligned. They remind me that leadership is not about titles or recognition; it's about influence rooted in compassion and truth.

That doesn't mean everyone will like how you lead. In fact, being anchored in your values may cause discomfort for others. Some won't agree with your choices, some may misinterpret your intentions, and some won't like you. And that's okay. When your values are clear, you don't have to be everyone's favorite - you have to be consistent.

Because here's the truth: when you know what you stand for, you won't fall for what doesn't serve you. You won't chase validation or compromise your integrity to keep the peace. You'll learn that peace comes from alignment, not approval.

Anchored leadership transforms people - not by force, but by example. When your values are visible in your words and actions, people begin to trust you. They start to feel safe following your lead, not because you're flawless, but because you're authentic.

Leadership from the inside out means that your outer actions mirror your inner beliefs. It's a form of integrity that radiates calm confidence. You don't need to shout your values to the rooftops; you live them. And in doing so, you give others permission to do the same - to define themselves for themselves, just as Audre Lorde so powerfully said.

Anchoring your values is not a one-time exercise. It's a daily practice. A morning check-in, a quiet pause before a tough decision, a reflection at the end of the day. It's asking yourself:

- Did I lead from my center today?
- Did I honor what I believe in, even when it was hard?
- Did my actions reflect the person I want to be?

When you stay rooted in your answers, your leadership becomes not just practical - but transformational.

Because in the end, it's your values that hold you steady, that guide your light through the storm, and that define who you are long after the applause fades. To lead from the inside out is to lead from your anchor, and never to forget where it's rooted.

Self-Reflection Questions

When was the last time you made a decision that truly reflected your values, even when it was uncomfortable or unpopular? What did that moment teach you about your leadership?

Which of your core values feels the most tested in your current season of life, and how can you stay anchored to it more intentionally each day?

Day 7: Confidence and Walking in Your Power

"If you want to fly, you have to give up the things that weigh you down." ~ Toni Morrison

I firmly believe that we must experience a level of heaviness to understand what we need to let go of to become better or grow. The weight teaches us where freedom lives. It's easy to think that growth is only about adding more skills, more recognition, more accomplishments - but often, the real transformation happens when we release what no longer serves us.

In leadership, that heaviness often comes from invisible expectations. They come from all directions...our direct reports, our peers, our leaders, and even those silently observing from the sidelines. Each voice, each perspective, each unspoken expectation can slowly begin to pile on. Without realizing it, we start measuring our worth by how others see us rather than how we see ourselves.

For me, this became a quiet, exhausting chase for validation. I wanted to be seen as a respectable leader who worked hard and cared deeply. I wanted everyone to like me, to see that my intentions were good and that I was worthy of their respect. What I didn't understand at the time was that such a goal could never be achieved. No matter how hard you work, no matter how genuine your heart is, there will always be someone who doesn't see you in the light you

26

hope for.

It took time - and pain - for me to realize this truth. I started noticing that while some people who reported to me admired my leadership, others questioned it. Some leaders above me offered support and encouragement, while others remained distant or dismissive. At first, I internalized it all. Each act of indifference felt personal. Every whisper of critique became another weight added to my shoulders.

Soon, those weights began to alter how I saw myself. Presentations that once brought me joy now filled me with anxiety. Meetings that once energized me began to drain me. I felt my confidence slipping, replaced by a fear that I was no longer enough. I developed insecurities that had never existed before. And over time, I realized that I was no longer walking in my power - I was walking under the weight of others' opinions.

But one day, something in me shifted. I got tired of feeling small. Tired of shrinking in spaces I had once dreamed of being in. I sat down, opened a notebook, and started writing every weight that had been holding me down. I listed my fears, my doubts, my insecurities, and the names or situations that had quietly chipped away at my confidence. Then I crossed each one out, line by line. It was my way of releasing what didn't belong to me anymore.

That exercise was symbolic - but powerful. It marked the beginning of my return to myself. I made a promise to stay the course of doing my absolute best, regardless of who noticed or who didn't. I recommitted to my mission and reminded myself that leadership was never about being liked; it was about being aligned.

The moment I let go of the weight, something incredible happened: I started to fly. Doors of opportunity began to open. One I had been knocking on for years without success. My inbox is filled with requests from employees asking for mentorship. Invitations came for speaking engagements. My presence was recognized, not because I was trying to prove my worth, but because I was walking in it.

Toni Morrison's words became my lived truth: "If you want to fly, you have to give up the things that weigh you down." Confidence doesn't come from pretending to have it all together; it comes from the courage to let go. To release the need for validation. To shed the layers of fear that once made you question your greatness. When you do that, you don't just walk in your power - you rise in it.

As leaders, we carry a lot. The responsibility, the pressure, the expectations - they don't disappear. But what can change is how we carry them. When we lead from a place of self-awareness and alignment, the load feels lighter. We stop carrying what isn't ours, and in doing so, we make space for clarity, peace, and purpose.

Walking in your power doesn't mean you'll never feel fear again - it means you'll no longer let it hold you hostage. It means you keep showing up, grounded in your truth, and leading from the inside out.

Self-Reflection Questions

What "weights" have you been carrying that no longer serve your growth?

How might letting go create more space for your confidence to soar?

Day 8: Resilience - Bouncing Back Stronger

"The ultimate measure of a man is not where he stands in moments of comfort and convenience, but where he stands at times of challenge and controversy." ~ Dr. Martin Luther King Jr.

The first time I experienced trauma in the workplace with a toxic leader, it was entirely new for me. I had always prided myself on professionalism and self-control, so I did what I had always done - held it together at work. On the outside, I appeared calm and composed. But behind closed doors, it tore me apart. I found myself crying late at night, struggling to sleep, and replaying every conversation in my mind. I felt anxious, rejected, confused, and angry. I couldn't understand how someone in a leadership position could operate from such a destructive place, nor why I had become a target of that behavior.

That season left me questioning my worth and wondering what I could have done differently. But it also planted a seed - a seed that would later grow into awareness, wisdom, and resilience. I didn't know it then, but that painful experience was shaping the leader I would one day become.

When I encountered toxicity a second time, it was in a completely different environment, but the signs were familiar. The same tension. The same subtle control tactics. The same quiet erosion of trust. Only this time, I recognized it early. I could sense the same emotional undercurrent that had once blindsided me.

The difference was me. I was no longer that same unguarded version of myself. I had matured, learned to trust my intuition, and built a toolkit for handling difficult people and situations. I leaned into therapy, practiced deep breathing, prayed, meditated, and confided in a trusted family member who could help me process the details with clarity and compassion.

Through these practices, I found the strength I didn't know I had. I began to separate their behavior from my identity. I realized it wasn't a reflection of my inadequacy - it was a reflection of their inner conflict. The moment I made that distinction, everything shifted. I stopped internalizing the negativity and started focusing on my peace.

Interestingly, as time went on, others began to share their own experiences with that same person - unsolicited - and their stories aligned with mine. That confirmation brought a quiet relief. I wasn't imagining it, and I wasn't alone. It reaffirmed that my observations were valid and that I could trust my discernment.

When leaders find themselves in toxic work cultures, the best thing we can do is remain steadfast in doing what is right - all the time. We can't always control how others treat us, but we can control how we respond.

As someone who values compassion and integrity, I learned to resist the urge to retaliate or mirror poor behavior. Instead, I focused on maintaining professionalism, protecting my peace, and showing up in alignment with my values.

It's easy to take things personally when you're under attack or being misunderstood, but often the toxicity of others stems from an unresolved internal battle. Misery loves company - but you don't have to accept the invitation.

The power of resilience is found in your ability to choose how you show up in the face of adversity. Lead yourself well by taking care of your mind, body, and spirit. Set boundaries that protect your energy. Do the things that keep you grounded - whether that's journaling, meditation and prayer, walking, or connecting with people who speak life into you.

Every time we overcome a season of adversity, we are being prepared for something greater. Resilience isn't just about recovering from hardship - it's about transforming through it. Each challenge reveals new depths of strength, empathy, and purpose within us.

Looking back, I can see how each painful experience refined my leadership. The first time, I broke down. The second time, I broke through. The next time, I will rise with even more wisdom, emotional stability, and clarity about who I am and how I lead.

The key is to use your resources and to be intentional about your healing. Therapy, faith, reflection, and trusted relationships are not signs of weakness - they are tools of strength. They help you remain resilient when life or leadership gets heavy.

Through it all, the lesson remains consistent: every challenge is an opportunity to become wiser, more grounded, and more resourceful - not just for yourself, but for others who will one day face similar storms. Resilience is not the absence of pain; it's the presence of purpose in the midst of it.

So when life presents you with another difficult chapter, remember - you've already proven you can rise. You've already built the strength to withstand it. This time, you won't just bounce back; you'll bounce forward, stronger than ever before.

Self-Reflection Questions

When faced with toxic or challenging environments, what practices help you stay grounded and aligned with your core values?

How can you transform past pain or adversity into wisdom that strengthens your leadership and supports others around you?

Day 9: Energy - Protecting Your Mental & Emotional Space

"You have power over your mind - not outside events. Realize this, and you will find strength." ~ Marcus Aurelius

For a long time, I believed strength meant endurance. If something felt heavy, uncomfortable, or emotionally draining, I told myself it was simply part of leadership. I learned how to stay composed, show up prepared, and perform well regardless of what was happening internally. On the outside, I appeared steady. On the inside, I was learning - often the hard way - that not every space deserves full access to your mental and emotional energy.

Protecting my mental and emotional space did not come naturally to me. It was learned through moments of exhaustion, confusion, and deep self-reflection. I had to come to terms with the reality that being resilient without discernment can quietly lead to self-abandonment. Leadership, especially when done with integrity and heart, requires presence. And presence cannot be sustained when your inner world is constantly under attack.

One of the most important lessons I learned was how to detect what is good and what is not - not just on paper, but in practice. I began paying attention to how I felt before, during, and after interactions. Some people and environments energized me, sharpened my thinking, and expanded my capacity to lead well. Others left me second-guessing myself, feeling diminished, or emotionally drained. The difference was subtle at first, but once I learned to notice it, I could no longer ignore it.

I realized that negativity does not always announce itself loudly. Sometimes it hides behind sarcasm, passive-aggressive comments, control masked as concern, or leadership styles that value results over people. I learned that just because something is normalized does not mean it is healthy. And just because someone holds authority does not mean they are safe to follow closely.

As I grew in self-awareness, I also grew in responsibility. I could no longer blame environments alone for how I felt. I had to take ownership of my proximity - who I allowed access to my thoughts, emotions, and time. That meant making difficult decisions. Sometimes it meant removing myself from conversations, relationships, or spaces that consistently felt negative or misaligned with my values, not out of anger or avoidance, but out of wisdom.

Removing myself was not quitting. It was choosing preservation over depletion.

At the same time, I learned that protection does not always mean retreat. There were moments when I recognized that I had the emotional capacity, authority, and clarity to stay and be the catalyst for change. Leadership from the inside out requires discernment - not every room needs to be exited, and not every room needs to be fixed. But some rooms need a shift, and sometimes you are the one equipped to initiate it.

I learned how to read the room. To sense when negativity was rooted in fear, burnout, or misalignment rather than malice. In those moments, I chose to lead differently - to bring calm instead of chaos, clarity instead of confusion, and compassion instead of criticism. I learned that energy is contagious, and so is leadership. When one person chooses to respond rather than react, to listen rather than assume, the atmosphere can change.

But even that required boundaries.

Being a catalyst does not mean absorbing everything. It means anchoring yourself so deeply in who you are that the room cannot decide how you show up. I had to learn how to enter spaces grounded, not guarded - aware, not anxious. I learned to pause before responding, to ask better questions, and to disengage when conversations became unproductive or harmful. Protecting my energy meant knowing when to speak, when to stay silent, and when to walk away.

This journey reshaped how I view leadership. Leadership is not only about influence over others; it is about stewardship of self. You cannot lead people well if you are constantly mentally exhausted, emotionally triggered, or spiritually disconnected. Protecting your inner world is not selfish - it is strategic. It is foundational.

Today, I am far more intentional about where I invest my energy. I choose environments that align with my values and people who value growth, accountability, and respect. I no longer feel the need to explain every boundary or justify every decision. I trust the discernment I have developed. I understand that peace is not something to be negotiated away for acceptance or approval.

Leading from the inside out means honoring the signals your mind and body give you. It means recognizing when something is off and having the courage to respond accordingly. Sometimes that response is removal. Sometimes it is reform. But it is always rooted in self-awareness and self-respect.

Protecting my mental and emotional space has made me a better leader, not a distant one. A clearer one. A healthier one. It has allowed me to lead with intention rather than impulse, with strength rather than survival. And it has taught me this enduring truth: when you protect what is happening within you, you lead with a power that no environment can take away.

Self-Reflection Questions

What boundaries can you set to protect your mental and emotional energy when faced with challenging people or environments?

How can you shift from reacting to negativity to responding with grounded peace and clarity?

Day 10: Courage Over Fear - Do It Afraid

"I learned that courage was not the absence of fear, but the triumph over it." ~
Nelson Mandela

As leaders, we must learn to do it afraid. Courage is not the absence of fear - it's
the decision to move forward despite it. Early in my career, fear often stood in
my way. I was afraid of public speaking, of making mistakes, of stepping into
spaces where I didn't feel fully prepared or qualified. Each fear chipped away
at my confidence and limited my ability to lead myself effectively. I showed
up to work, but not always with the boldness or assurance that authentic
leadership requires.

That all changed when I was given an opportunity that stretched me far beyond
my comfort zone. I was asked to lead the largest team I had ever led — over
150 employees — in an environment completely unfamiliar to me. The team
worked in a space I hadn't led before, and to make it even more intimidating,
most of the employees spoke a language I didn't. I remember feeling nervous,
uncertain, and even unqualified. But something inside me whispered: Do it
afraid.

One of the greatest myths in leadership is that we must have deep expertise in
every space we lead. While understanding the work is essential, true leadership
is not just about knowledge - it's about people. It's about the willingness to
listen, learn, and build trust even when you don't have all the answers.

When I first stepped into that new leadership role, I made what I now see as a common mistake: I led with a plan before I led with connection. I quickly developed a strategy and brought the supervisors together to discuss how we would move the team forward. I was excited and confident in the plan, but when I presented it, I was met with silence. Blank stares. No engagement. It was clear my approach had missed the mark.

Later, one of the team members courageously pulled me aside and said, "We don't know you yet. You came in with a plan before taking the time to understand how we work." That truth hit me hard — but it was exactly what I needed to hear.

As leaders, we must be willing to receive feedback with humility and act on it. That conversation became a turning point for me. I realized that fear had caused me to overcompensate — to hide behind strategy and structure instead of connection and curiosity. I had been trying to prove myself instead of simply being myself and learning from the people who already had the expertise I lacked.

I took that feedback to heart. I began to spend time with the team — walking the floor, observing, listening, and asking questions. I asked employees to show me how they did their work and what challenges they faced. I didn't pretend to know everything; I admitted what I didn't realize and expressed genuine curiosity.

In those moments, something powerful began to shift. My fear started to fade, and my confidence grew — not from mastering the technical side of the work, but from building authentic relationships. I discovered that vulnerability was not a weakness but a bridge. When I allowed myself to be real and human, others opened up too. The more I listened, the more trust developed, and the more united our team became.

Through that experience, I learned that courage doesn't always look bold or loud. Sometimes, courage looks like humility. It's having the strength to say, I don't know, but I'm willing to learn. It's choosing connection over control, people over process, and growth over perfection.

Over time, the team's performance began to shift. Engagement improved, communication opened up, and results followed. But the most powerful transformation wasn't just in metrics — it was in mindset. As I learned to lead courageously, others began to follow suit.

Courage is contagious. When leaders model it, it spreads through the team like a quiet but steady fire. People start taking initiative, sharing ideas, and approaching challenges without fear of failure. They begin to feel safe — and when people feel safe, they thrive.

Doing it afraid taught me that courage and fear can coexist. The goal isn't to eliminate fear but to keep moving through it with intention and faith. The same fear that once made me question my ability became the very force that fueled my growth. Every new challenge since then has reminded me of that season — that courage is a muscle, and the only way to strengthen it is to keep exercising it.

As leaders, we will always face moments that test our confidence, stretch our limits, and invite self-doubt. But the true mark of leadership is not perfection — it's perseverance. When fear arises, remember this: you are capable, you are equipped, and you can do it afraid.

Self-Reflection Questions

What fear has been holding you back from stepping fully into your leadership potential?

What practical steps can you take this week to "do it afraid" and lead with courage rather than hesitation?

II

Part II: Growing in Practice

Awareness becomes meaningful through action. This section focuses on applying what you've uncovered internally and translating insight into consistent behaviors, choices, and habits. Growth happens in the everyday moments where intention meets practice and leadership is refined through experience.

Day 11: Doing the Work Daily - The Discipline of Growth

"You don't make progress by standing on the sidelines, whimpering and complaining. You make progress by implementing ideas." ~ Shirley Chisholm

Many people admire the outcome of hard work—the promotion, recognition, and visible success. What they rarely see is the preparation that came earlier: late nights, doubts, and long stretches where progress felt invisible. These are the grit years — when commitment is tested, and you keep showing up with no results in sight.

Growth doesn't occur during applause. It happens in the unglamorous spaces of consistency—when no one notices and giving up feels easier. Those moments shape us. The work behind the scenes develops the strength needed for authentic, enduring leadership.

There's something powerful about showing up daily, even when you don't feel like it. Doing the work, especially when it's inconvenient, builds discipline. Discipline turns potential into progress and ideas into impact. Leaders who do the work, regardless of recognition, eventually let consistency speak for itself. Others trust them because they've proven, first to themselves, that they're reliable.

But discipline is not perfection — it's persistence. It's not about doing everything every day, but about doing something every day to move toward who you want to become. Lead yourself intentionally before leading others.

A daily rhythm helps, and it looks different for everyone. I don't use a rigid framework—I'm flexible and responsive—but my foundation stays the same: reflection, intentional action, and review.

For me, reflection begins with morning meditation. A quiet moment helps organize my thoughts before the noise of leadership, whether you reflect in bed, on a walk, or while exercising, that stillness sets your mindset and priorities.

Next, set intentions. Write down at least one thing you'll accomplish today. I tell myself, "I will," not "I can." That language shift, from a life coach, turns possibility into commitment. Saying "I will" trains your mind to act with purpose rather than wait for permission.

Set realistic goals for your current season. On busy days, I pick one goal I can accomplish. On lighter days, I might add more. Consistency, not quantity, matters most. Confidence builds one completed promise at a time.

Then, make time for what matters. Goals are only as strong as the space you give them. Discipline is carving out and protecting time for your commitments. At day's end, reflect: How did I do? What worked? What could improve tomorrow?

This rhythm—reflection, intention, review—keeps you anchored in purpose and flexible for growth. It's not about perfect execution but being present.

For leaders, discipline is essential. Discipline anchors our actions as motivation fades. It shapes integrity, fosters self-leadership, and develops patience, structure, accountability, and emotional resilience for effective leadership in uncertainty.

Daily consistency makes you a model of reliability. People follow consistency before charisma. They trust leaders who live their values, not just talk about them.

Finding your rhythm isn't about copying others. Discover practices that ground you. Some leaders thrive on routines; others flourish with spontaneous reflection and creativity. Most important is the commitment to show up for yourself daily.

Breakthroughs rarely come in grand moments—they unfold in disciplined, consistent effort. Over time, invisible work produces visible growth. The consistent leader stands in the light by result, not luck.

Keep doing the work—even unseen. Show up with intention. Lead yourself daily; how you show up for yourself determines how you'll show up for others. That's the discipline that grows leaders from the inside out.

Self-Reflection Questions

Where in your life or leadership have you been relying on motivation instead of daily discipline to move forward?

What is one daily habit, if practiced with discipline, that would create the most significant long-term impact in how you lead yourself and others?

Day 12: Guarding Your Peace

"Never be in a hurry; do everything quietly and in a calm spirit. Do not lose your inner peace for anything whatsoever." ~ Harriet Tubman

Let's talk about one of the most significant focus areas for any human being - especially for those who lead: peace. Your peace is too important, too valuable, and too expensive to be bought. It is the core that keeps you grounded when life feels chaotic and uncertain. It provides the clarity and direction that guide your thoughts, actions, and decisions. Peace is the quiet strength that allows you to show up authentically, no matter what is happening around you. It's your North Star - the steady light that helps you navigate both calm and stormy seasons.

When we are at peace, we think clearly. We respond instead of react. We move with intention instead of impulse. But to maintain this place of internal calm, we must first recognize what threatens it. The truth is, peace doesn't just happen - it must be guarded. Some barriers and distractions limit our ability to dwell in a peaceful place, often in subtle ways.

Some of these barriers come disguised as good things - like the desire to help others or to meet expectations. Being a "yes" person can feel noble at first, but over time, it depletes your energy and divides your focus. When we say yes to everything, we're often saying no to ourselves - no to rest, no to reflection, no to what we actually need. Peace requires discernment. You have to know when to give and when to step back.

Another peace thief is remaining in toxic environments - spaces that drain more than they deposit. Whether it's a workplace culture, a relationship, or even a mindset, toxicity disrupts your sense of balance. Guarding your peace means having the courage to make changes that align with your emotional and mental well-being. Sometimes that means walking away, and other times it means staying - but staying differently, with boundaries and awareness.

Comparison is another silent enemy. The moment we start measuring our progress against others, peace begins to slip away. We lose focus on our unique journey and start chasing validation instead of purpose. The only person you need to outgrow is the version of yourself from yesterday. Peace grows when we learn to celebrate others without questioning our own worth.

Unresolved emotions also disturb peace. The feelings we suppress don't disappear; they hide, waiting to resurface in moments of stress or conflict. Healing is part of protecting peace. Reflection, journaling, therapy, prayer, and honest conversations are ways to release what we've carried too long. Letting go is not weakness - it's wisdom. It's saying, "I refuse to let what hurt me continue to rule me."

Then there are the external distractions - social media, other people's opinions, and the constant noise that surrounds us daily. The more we consume, the harder it becomes to hear ourselves. Guarding peace sometimes looks like logging off, turning down the volume, and reclaiming your focus. You don't need every opinion, every update, or every notification. You need space to breathe, think, and be.

Peace allows us the mental space and capacity to reflect on what we're learning as we navigate both our personal and professional lives. It offers a place of solitude that doesn't require validation or applause. It's in this quiet space that confirmation happens - the "aha" moments, the clarity of thought, and the courage to make the decisions we once delayed.

Some of the best ideas are born in moments of stillness. When the noise quiets down, creativity rises. When the pressure lifts, direction becomes clear. Peace doesn't just bring calm - it brings clarity. It helps us recognize growth in all stages and seasons of life. And as leaders, that clarity is invaluable.

Guarding your peace is not selfish - it's strategic. It's an act of leadership, a declaration that says, "I will not lead from emptiness." Because when your peace is disturbed, your judgment is clouded. When you're constantly over-whelmed, it's hard to inspire confidence or compassion in others. Protecting your peace allows you to lead from overflow, not exhaustion.

So, what does guarding your peace look like in practice? It looks like setting boundaries without guilt. It looks like resting even when the world tells you to grind. It seems like being intentional about what you allow into your mind and spirit - what you watch, what you listen to, and who you surround yourself with. It looks like being still, not as a sign of weakness, but as a sign of wisdom.

Peace is not passive; it's powerful. It's the space where vision becomes clearer, strength becomes renewed, and alignment takes root. The more you protect your peace, the more effective and fulfilled you become - not just as a leader, but as a human being.

So, take inventory. Ask yourself: What consistently disturbs my peace, and why do I allow it space in my life? Then, make one intentional change this week to reclaim that peace. Guard it fiercely. Nurture it daily. Because your peace is not a luxury - it's a necessity.

And the truth is, no one else can protect it for you.

Self-Reflection Questions

What daily habits or relationships most impact your sense of peace - positively or negatively?

In what ways can you strengthen your boundaries to protect your peace – while still leading effectively?

Day 13: Leading with Heart & Wisdom

"A good head and a good heart are always a formidable combination." ~ Nelson Mandela

As leaders, it is essential to have emotional intelligence - the ability to understand ourselves and others in a way that strengthens relationships, fosters collaboration, and drives purpose. I learned this early on in my career while working with people from all walks of life, with diverse cultural backgrounds and experiences. Emotional intelligence is more than a leadership skill - it's a leadership posture. It's how we approach people, how we listen, and how we respond, especially when the environment challenges our credibility or our capacity.

There was a season in my leadership journey where I led a team that was more senior than I was - individuals with deep institutional knowledge, long tenure, and a mastery of the work. I was new to the space, and while I brought a wealth of leadership experience, I lacked the technical expertise that many of them had. That gap did not go unnoticed. Some questioned my knowledge and authority. Others silently tested my resolve. In moments like that, emotional intelligence isn't optional - it becomes essential.

Initially, I was asked to step in temporarily, to "fill in the gaps" for a leadership role expected to last only two months. Two months turned into a year. The longer I stayed, the more pressure I felt. Every idea I offered seemed to meet resistance. Every suggestion was followed by skepticism. There were days it would have been easier to retreat, to operate defensively, or to try to prove myself louder than the doubt around me. But instead, I chose to lead with heart and wisdom rather than ego and frustration.

I decided to slow down and see my team before trying to lead them. I spent intentional time with each person one-on-one; not to evaluate, but to understand. I wanted to know their wants, worries, and wins - what motivated them, what discouraged them, and what they were most proud of. That investment of time became my turning point.

What I discovered was that people open up when they feel seen. They trust when they feel understood. And they commit when they feel valued. Through that process, I became more self-aware - not just about what I brought to the table, but about how my emotions, tone, and body language impacted the room.

That self-awareness helped me remain steady even when tension surfaced. I learned that emotional intelligence isn't about suppressing emotion - it's about mastering your response to it. I had to model patience when deadlines got tight, humility when I didn't know the answer, and courage when decisions weren't popular.

Over time, something shifted. The same team that once questioned me began to collaborate more openly. They started coming to me for perspective, asking for input, and seeking alignment. That trust wasn't built overnight - it was earned through consistency, empathy, and transparency.

Through that experience, I realized that leadership isn't about having all the answers - it's about creating an environment where people feel safe enough to share theirs. My responsibility was not to outshine anyone, but to illuminate the path forward so everyone could thrive together.

It also taught me humility - the reminder that a leader's strength lies not only in vision, but in their ability to listen, to learn, and to let others lead where they are strongest. When we lead from the heart, we invite others to bring their whole selves to the table. When we lead with wisdom, we guide that collective energy toward purpose and impact.

Emotional intelligence sits at the intersection of both. It's the bridge that connects understanding with action. It allows us to see the person before the problem, to respond thoughtfully rather than react impulsively, and to model the kind of grounded leadership that transforms cultures, not just processes.

When leaders prioritize people - truly knowing their stories, strengths, and struggles - decision-making becomes more organic. Culture becomes more inclusive. And trust becomes the currency that sustains success. That is the heart and wisdom of leadership - to lead not from position, but from compassion, curiosity, and courage.

Self-Reflection Questions

How do I respond when my authority or knowledge is challenged - with defensiveness, or with curiosity and empathy?

In what ways can I better understand the wants, worries, and wins of the people I lead?

Day 14: Leading Without Masks - The Power of Authentic Leadership

"We have to dare to be ourselves, however frightening or strange that self may prove to be. ~ Audre Lorde

There is power in authenticity - in showing up as your whole self, unfiltered and unmasked. Too often, leaders wear masks to fit into expectations that were never meant for them. The mask might look like confidence when we're unsure, like control when we're overwhelmed, or like silence when we really want to speak the truth. But every time we wear those masks, we drift a little further away from the essence of who we are - and from the kind of leader we were meant to be.

As leaders, the pressure to perform is constant. Sometimes those expectations come from others - colleagues, senior leaders, or even cultural norms about what leadership should look like. Other times, they come from within - the voice that whispers you have to be stronger, smarter, or tougher to be respected. These pressures slowly shape a version of us that feels "safe" but isn't real. The mask forms when we try to live up to someone's definition of leadership rather than lead from our truth.

There was a time in my own career when being authentic didn't seem to make sense. I believed that showing vulnerability could be misunderstood - that people might see my kindness as weakness or interpret my openness as a lack of authority. I thought I had to present a perfect image to gain respect, that I had to have all the answers to be seen as capable. But that belief came from fear, not strength. It came from trying to manage perception rather than deepen connection.

The turning point came when I decided to be me. I started sharing my real experiences – not just my wins, but my failures and lessons. I admitted when I didn't know something, and I asked for help when I needed it. I allowed my team to see the human behind the title. And something powerful happened – connection replaced distance. Trust grew. The environment shifted from guarded professionalism to genuine collaboration. My team no longer followed because they had to; they followed because they wanted to.

Authenticity is freeing. It releases us from the exhausting performance of perfection. When you are true to yourself, you give others silent permission to do the same – to bring their whole selves, with all their brilliance and flaws, to the work. People feel safe to contribute, to innovate, to speak honestly. They see that their leader doesn't need to pretend, and neither do they.

The masks we wear are not always malicious; sometimes, they're protective. We put them on to appear more confident than we feel, to seem more knowledgeable, or to hide insecurities we fear others might notice. But over time, those masks harden. They begin to separate us from the people we lead. Leadership becomes about image management instead of impact. And when that happens, we lose the ability to connect at the heart level – the level where actual influence and growth occur.

Authenticity doesn't mean oversharing or losing professionalism. It means aligning what you say, what you do, and what you believe – consistently. It means leading from your values even when it's uncomfortable, and allowing your humanity to guide your leadership. Authentic leadership is not about being perfect; it's about being present – honest, self-aware, and courageous enough to lead from truth.

When we dare to remove the mask, something remarkable happens. We stop leading from ego and start leading from empathy. We stop trying to control how others see us and start focusing on how we can serve them. We admit mistakes rather than hide them, and we model what accountability looks like. We lead with humility and still hold confidence. That balance - humility with strength - is what makes authenticity magnetic.

The more I led from that place, the more I realized that vulnerability is not weakness; it's wisdom. It's the courage to say, "I'm growing too." It's the awareness that leadership is not a performance - it's a partnership. When we own our truth and let others see it, we build something much more profound than authority - we build trust.

And trust, once built, becomes the foundation for every great team, every innovative idea, and every meaningful outcome. When you lead without masks, you create space for others to breathe, learn, and lead authentically, too. That is the kind of leadership that lasts - leadership rooted in truth, sustained by empathy, and grounded in purpose.

Self-Reflection Questions

What "mask" do I find myself wearing most often as a leader, and what fear might it be protecting?

How can I practice authenticity more boldly - leading from my values rather than from others' expectations?

Day 15: Living Aligned With Your Why

"Purpose is an incredible alarm clock." ~ Myles Munroe

I was a young adult when I first understood what it meant to live life on purpose. Over twenty years ago, I picked up a book that would change the way I saw my entire existence: The Purpose Driven Life by Rick Warren. I didn't know it then, but that book would plant the first seed of what purpose-driven leadership would eventually mean to me. It opened my eyes to something simple yet revolutionary: that I didn't have to live within the limits the world, culture, or even family tradition silently imposed on me. I could live beyond "normal." I could live beyond expectations. I could choose a purpose.

At that time, I was in college, and although I had an idea of the type of work I wanted to do, I wasn't confident about the path I would take to get there. What I did know was that I wanted to help people improve their lives. It was general, broad, and unstructured - but it was real. Majoring in psychology and working in corporate America while I was still in school helped me slowly shape that vision. I discovered something consistent about myself: my heart was always drawn to people. Not their titles. Not their achievements. People.

There was something deeply meaningful to me about being in a position to help someone see themselves differently - a little more clearly, a little more boldly, a little more compassionately. Every small interaction I had with strangers, classmates, coworkers, or friends reaffirmed that I cared about helping people look at themselves through a better lens. I wanted them to

56

see their own greatness, even when they couldn't recognize it. That instinct - to lift, guide, encourage, and inspire - wasn't something I had to force. It was something that flowed out of me. It was part of my why long before I had language for it.

My first official leadership role came a few years after reading that book, but in reality, I had been leading long before that moment. I was the oldest sister of four younger sisters, a natural "big sister mode" leader who stepped in, guided, mediated, and supported without being asked. In my social circles, I was always the one planning the events, hosting the conversations, and walking friends through relationship challenges or life decisions. Leadership showed up in my life before I ever applied for a job that required it. And through prayer and my spiritual journey, I was repeatedly reminded of what others often reflected to me: that leadership wasn't just something I did. It was who I was.

Over the years, I found myself in roles that allowed me to lead formally - managing teams, guiding cultures, building people up, and being entrusted with responsibilities that stretched me. Every promotion, every recognition, every moment of influence felt humbling. It wasn't about the spotlight; it was about the confirmation that I was aligned. I was living on purpose. I was operating inside the very thing God placed in me.

But purpose, I've learned, doesn't always feel glamorous. There were many seasons where alignment didn't feel like applause - it felt like endurance. I walked through challenges that could have made me question everything: low pay despite knowing my value, leaders who lacked compassion or integrity, toxic work environments, unruly direct reports, and roles that looked promising at first but turned into dead ends. There were days when I wanted to give up, walk away, or shrink myself so I wouldn't be disappointed again.

And yet, every time I got quiet, every time I reflected, every time I prayed, the same confirmation rose to the surface: stay aligned. Sometimes alignment meant pushing through. Other times, it meant redirecting myself. Both required courage. Both required trust. Both required me to listen to my inner voice even when my circumstances didn't make sense.

Living aligned with your why is not about feeling good all the time. It's about being anchored – so anchored that even when you're tired, unsure, or frustrated, something inside of you still nudges you to keep going. Something inside of you still reminds you that you're meant for this. Something inside of you still whispers, "This is what you were created to do."

For me, that whisper has always been tied to people. Encouraging, guiding, seeing, and motivating them. Even on days when my own energy was low, even when I was navigating my own storms, I found myself pouring into others because it was simply who I am. Purpose doesn't turn off because life gets hard. Alignment doesn't take a break because circumstances shift. When something is in you, it expresses itself naturally – good, bad, or indifferent.

This is what I want every leader reading this to understand: Your why is not something outside of you. It's something already inside you. It shows up in your instincts. It shows up in what breaks your heart. It shows up in what energizes you. It shows up in the moments when no one is watching. Purpose is less about a title and more about a truth. A truth about who you are and what you uniquely bring into the world.

Living aligned with your why means honoring that truth. It means leading from your conviction, not from comparison. It means operating from intention, not impression. It means showing up as the fullest version of yourself, even when it challenges old patterns, old fears, or old expectations. Alignment requires honesty – brutal, compassionate honesty with yourself about what feels right and what feels forced.

If you pay attention, alignment speaks early. You'll feel it before you can describe it. You'll know when you've drifted from your why because you'll feel unsettled, irritated, disconnected, or resentful. And you'll see when you're living aligned because peace finds you - even in the middle of pressure. Clarity comes. Confidence rises. Things that once felt heavy begin to feel possible again.

The truth is, alignment doesn't exempt you from challenges, but it gives you the resilience to move through them. It doesn't eliminate obstacles, but it gives you the wisdom to navigate around them. It doesn't guarantee an easy journey, but it guarantees a meaningful one.

Looking back, I can see that every step of my journey - every leadership opportunity, every challenging experience, every moment of doubt, every confirmation - was preparing me for the work I'm doing now. Leading from the inside out. Guiding people from their truth instead of their fear. Helping them reconnect with their own why so they can lead with authenticity and courage.

Because when you understand your why, you stop chasing validation and start walking in purpose. You stop performing and start becoming. You stop surviving leadership and start transforming through it.

Your why is your anchor. Your compass. Your reminder that everything you need to lead with power, peace, and intention is already within you.

Self-Reflection Questions

How do I consistently make people feel through my words, decisions, and presence - especially when no one is watching?

What slight, intentional shift can I make today that aligns my daily behavior more closely with the leader I aspire to be?

Day 16: Gratitude - Finding Strength in Appreciation

"He is a wise man who does not grieve for the things which he has not, but rejoices for those which he has." ~ Epictetus

Gratitude is one of the most underestimated sources of power we have on our journey. With all the challenges we overcome - personally, professionally, emotionally - there is one truth that continually grounds me: growth is not found in the destination; it is shaped in the journey. And the only way we truly honor that journey is by practicing gratitude along the way.

When I look back over the many seasons of my life, I realize how much my perspective has been shaped by appreciation. I'm grateful not only for where I've ended up, but for every step, every pause, every setback, and every breakthrough that led me there. Gratitude changes how we perceive growth. It shifts our focus from what is missing to what is present, from what is wrong to what is working, and from comparison with others to alignment with ourselves.

So often we fall into the trap of believing that gratitude should only come once we "arrive". Once we accomplish the goal, secure the promotion, launch the business, or overcome the obstacle. But the fundamental transformation happens when we notice the value in the process. When we appreciate the small things and the big things - the lessons, the opportunities, the people, the clarity - we begin to see how every moment contributes to the outcome we're working toward.

I am grateful for every challenge I've experienced, not because it was easy, but because it shaped me. Difficulty has a way of grounding us. It brings us back to center and forces us to notice the strength we've gained, the wisdom we've earned, and the resilience we didn't realize we had. Gratitude isn't just about saying "thank you" for what's pleasant; it's about acknowledging that even the challenging experiences are part of our development.

One of the healthiest forms of gratitude is self-comparison - not against others, but against who you were yesterday. Gratitude keeps you focused on your own progress. It reminds you that your journey is uniquely yours and that growth is personal, not competitive. When you consistently look at your situation through a lens of appreciation, you quickly see what's working rather than what's lacking.

Being thankful for your current circumstances - even when they don't look like the final vision - is a discipline. It's an act of courage. It says, "I trust my direction. I honor my progress. I believe in what's unfolding." This mindset keeps you from rushing the process and allows you to experience it fully.

As we continue our journey of leading from the inside out, gratitude must extend beyond ourselves. It becomes a way of seeing the people around us - their efforts, their contributions, their growth. Whether we're leading a team, managing a business, supporting colleagues, or guiding family, appreciation is one of the most influential tools we have.

When people feel appreciated, they feel seen. And when they feel seen, they show up with more confidence, more energy, and more commitment. Gratitude builds trust. It strengthens loyalty. It creates an emotional safety that encourages people to take initiative, innovate, and bring their best.

This doesn't weaken your authority - in fact, it strengthens it. Practicing gratitude shows emotional intelligence. It demonstrates that you lead with awareness, compassion, and clarity. It also shows that you understand the human side of leadership: people need to feel valued, not just managed.

Gratitude is deeply connected to grace - the grace we give others when they make mistakes, and the grace we give ourselves when we stumble. No journey is linear. Growth will always include moments of starting over, resetting, pausing, and recalibrating. Gratitude helps us recognize that these moments are not failures; they are part of the transformation.

When we appreciate the lessons in our missteps, we don't get stuck in disappointment. We instead move forward with wisdom and clarity. Gratitude softens judgment and strengthens compassion, which is essential for emotional stability, mental wellness, and healthy leadership.

Gratitude doesn't have to be saved for significant milestones. It lives in the small, daily acknowledgments - the micro-moments that keep our mindset aligned with growth. A single thought, a shift in perspective, one small step forward, or even one task completed, is reason to pause and appreciate your progress.

The more intentional we are about gratitude, the more naturally it becomes part of who we are. Incorporate it into your routine:

- Reflect on one thing you're grateful for each day.
- Notice when something goes right, even if it's small.
- Acknowledge your effort, not just your results.
- Speak gratitude out loud - to yourself and others.

These simple practices keep gratitude at the forefront of your mind and make it a priority rather than an afterthought.

When people see you consistently practicing gratitude, it reflects strength, not weakness. They see someone grounded, present, emotionally aware, and mentally stable - someone who leads with both heart and wisdom. Gratitude shapes your presence. It influences how people feel around you. It makes others want to work with you, learn from you, and contribute to the environments you create.

At its core, gratitude is a form of mental and emotional wellness. It stabilizes your perspective, supports your mindset, and gives you the capacity to move toward your goals with intention and resilience. It allows you to lead yourself - and others - with clarity and authenticity.

Gratitude is not a soft skill; it is a strength-builder. It deepens your growth, reinforces your purpose, and elevates your leadership. When you move through life appreciating the process and the people, you unlock a level of internal alignment that no external accomplishment can give you.

As you continue leading from the inside out, let gratitude be one of your daily anchors. Let it reshape how you see your progress. Let it guide how you treat yourself and others. And most importantly, let it remind you that every step of your journey - even the imperfect ones - is part of your becoming.

Because gratitude is not just a feeling.

It is a choice.

A practice.

And one of the greatest strengths you can carry on your path.

<u>Self-Reflection Questions</u>

What is one challenge from your past that you can now view with gratitude because of how it shaped your growth?

How can you practice consistent, daily gratitude in a way that strengthens your leadership and your relationship with yourself?

Day 17: Adaptability - Thriving Through Change

"If the time is not ripe, we have to ripen the time." ~ Shirley Chisholm

Change is the only constant we can count on. No matter where we stand – in our careers, relationships, goals, or personal evolution – change will always find its way into our story. The ability to thrive through change is not an innate gift; it is a learned skill, one that strengthens us and expands our capacity to lead ourselves and others with confidence, steadiness, and vision.

Adaptability is the quiet leadership skill that separates those who survive seasons of transition from those who rise through them. It is what allows us to face the unpredictable with curiosity rather than fear. It makes navigating workplace, personal, and internal challenges easier because we stop resisting what is happening and start engaging with it.

My challenge to you – and the challenge I give myself – is to shift the way we perceive change. Instead of asking, "Why is this happening?" try asking, "What can I learn from this?"

Curiosity transforms change into opportunity. Rather than bracing ourselves for impact, we open ourselves to possibility. We look for lessons. We notice skills we can gain, strengths we can sharpen, and strategies we can improve. We begin to realize that every shift, whether welcomed or unexpected, carries a gift if we are willing to look for it.

When change becomes a teacher rather than a threat, adaptability becomes a natural part of our leadership and our lives.

Having worked multiple jobs across corporate America, I've learned that change is inevitable - sometimes celebrated, sometimes dreaded, but always present.

There were moments when changes were positive, bringing new opportunities, new leaders, new visions, or new directions for the work. Even in "good" change, adaptability is still required. A new opportunity can stretch your skills. A new leader can shift expectations. A new structure can redefine responsibilities. Growth, even when positive, calls for adjustment.

But then there were the harder shifts - reorganizations, reductions, restructures, and strategy pivots. I've lived through seasons when people around me lost their jobs, when uncertainty bred quiet fear, and when I questioned whether my own role would be affected. Those moments required not just skill, but courage. They demanded that I stay grounded enough to lead myself and steady enough to support others.

Adaptability in those seasons didn't mean ignoring fear or pretending everything was fine - it meant acknowledging the reality, accepting the change, and choosing how I wanted to show up through it.

One of the most critical responsibilities of leadership is owning the message of change. Whether you personally agree with the decision or not, when you communicate with your team, your energy becomes theirs.

If you're resistant, they'll resist. If you're anxious, they'll become anxious. If you're curious, calm, and grounded, they will feel safe enough to follow your lead.

Adapting to change is not about abandoning your opinions - it's about rising above them long enough to help others feel secure. People look to leaders for emotional guidance during transitions. This is why adaptability is not just a skill; it is a stabilizing force.

There are real consequences for resisting change. People who struggle with adaptability often:

- Complain instead of contributing.
- Cling to old methods even when they no longer work.
- Withdraw from collaboration.
- Produce less effective work.
- Carry frustration or negativity into their environment.

What begins as discomfort can turn into disengagement, which in turn affects workplace culture, team morale, and personal growth.

As leaders - or aspiring leaders - this is not the energy we want to carry. Resistance keeps us stuck. Adaptability moves us forward.

Adaptability doesn't only apply to corporate settings. If you run a business, lead a team, or serve clients, you already know that your success depends on your ability to pivot.

Customers' needs change.

Markets shift.

Business models evolve.

Strategies that once worked stop working.

Adaptive leaders see these shifts not as threats but as invitations to innovate.

They ask:

- What does this change require of me?
- How can I reposition myself or my team?
- What opportunity is hidden inside this shift?
- How can I support others through it?

When we are willing to adapt, we allow both ourselves and our organizations to remain relevant, creative, and future-focused.

One of the greatest lessons I've learned is that people who pivot well are often the ones most respected, admired, and trusted. Others look at them and ask, "How do you stay so calm?" But the truth is, calmness is not the absence of stress - it is the mastery of perspective.

Adaptability teaches you how to keep your internal world steady while your external world shifts. It helps you bounce back faster. It keeps you from getting stuck in frustration or fear. And most importantly, it allows you to reclaim your power in situations you cannot control.

People watch how you handle uncertainty. Your response becomes part of your leadership identity.

Every behavior begins with a belief. Adaptability starts in the mind long before it shows up in your actions. To thrive through change, you must intentionally shift from:

- Fear → Curiosity
- Rigidity → Flexibility
- Control → Openness
- Resistance → Acceptance
- Surviving → Growing

Once your mindset shifts, adaptability moves from being something you do to being part of who you are.

With that shift, your behavior changes. Your responses become more thoughtful. Your energy becomes calmer. Your leadership becomes stronger. And your influence becomes deeper.

When you embrace adaptability:

- You set the tone for your team.
- You reduce your own stress.
- You encourage creativity.
- You cultivate collaboration.
- You elevate workplace culture.
- You protect your mental well-being.
- You inspire others to pivot with confidence.

Adaptability is not just about adjusting to change - it is about leading through it. It is about navigating uncertainty with wisdom, courage, and emotional stability. It is the core of what makes leadership sustainable.

Change will continue to show up - sometimes invited, sometimes unexpected. But when you carry adaptability, you no longer brace yourself for the storm. You learn to move with it. You learn to learn from it. You learn to step into it with confidence rather than fear.

Thriving through change is not about controlling your environment - it's about mastering your inner world.

And when you can adapt with intention, you become the kind of leader others feel safe following. You become steady. You become resourceful. You become grounded.

You become powerful.

Self-Reflection Questions

What beliefs, habits, or roles am I holding onto that might be keeping me from evolving into my next level?

How do I typically respond to unexpected change, and what would it look like to respond from a place of curiosity instead of fear?

Day 18: Influence - Impact Without Force

"Power is not brute force and money; power is in your spirit. Power is in your soul."
~ Alice Walker

Influence is often misunderstood. Some believe influence is about telling people what to do or directing them toward a desired outcome. But real impact is not born from authority. It is not the volume of your voice, the title on your badge, or the power of your position.

Influence is an outcome.

It is the natural response people have to someone whose actions consistently reflect respect, trust, and alignment with their core values. It emerges when others feel seen, supported, and inspired - not manipulated, controlled, or coerced. Influence is the lasting imprint you leave on people long after the moment has passed.

I learned this early in my career, long before I ever saw myself as a leader.

I was working in a call center on the late-night shift. Those hours were slow, quiet, and often lonely. Leaders weren't usually present after hours, and it was common to go an entire shift without seeing a member of management walk the floor.

Except for one leader.

Every night, she would make her way out of her office and walk the floor, stopping to say hello as we were in between calls. She didn't do it for performance. She didn't do it for show. She genuinely wanted to connect. Some nights, she would ask how our evening was going. Other nights she'd ask about our families or check on someone she knew was having a tough week.

And then she'd return to her office - but she never closed her door.

I'd walk by and see employees quietly step to her doorway, peeking in to see if she was available. I'd watch people who had just finished a difficult call walk to her office, frustrated and come out calmer, sometimes even smiling. She was the kind of person who could make even the most hardened, short-tempered employee soften.

She made the "meanest" person smile. She made you feel like sunshine when you talked to her.

Nothing about her influence was forced.

One day, I learned that she would be my direct leader. And for the first time in my career, I experienced what it was like to have a leader who also became a mentor - someone who didn't just supervise me, but saw me. Someone who inspired me to grow both personally and professionally. Someone who spoke for me in rooms I wasn't in.

Her influence wasn't something she tried to have. It was something she embodied. Her presence alone created safety. Her consistency created trust. Her authenticity created admiration.

People gravitated toward her not because they had to, but because being around her made them better.

For years to come, she remained the same. Attentive. Open. Generous with her time. Courageous in conversation. Unshaken in integrity. And no matter who you asked - someone who worked closely with her or someone who only interacted with her once - they all had the same experience.

Everyone had a story about how she influenced them. Everyone had a moment where she coached, encouraged, or affirmed them in a way that shifted their career trajectory.

That's when I understood: **Influence isn't about getting people to follow you. Influence is about becoming someone worth following.**

From watching her, I learned the power of being vulnerable and authentic with people, yet still holding them accountable. She could correct you without making you feel small. She could give feedback without making you feel like you failed. Instead, you walked away feeling coached, supported, and inspired to rise to your own potential.

She taught me that being a leader isn't about taking people where you want them to go - it's about guiding them toward where they already desire to be. Influence connects with people's natural goodness. It amplifies it.

She never had to force anything. Not followership. Not performance. Not respect.

People willingly chose to be guided by her because her leadership made them feel capable, grounded, and valued.

Her example shaped the leader I committed to becoming:

The kind of leader who leaves people better than I found them.

The kind of leader who serves.

The kind of leader who sees.

The kind of leader whose impact is felt, not pushed.

Influence is not force.

It is present.

It is integrity.

It is alignment.

It is a connection.

Influence is the quiet, steady way you show up every day - and the way people remember you long after you're gone.

Self-Reflection Questions

Who has influenced your leadership style without using force, and what specific behaviors made their impact meaningful to you?

In what ways can you show up more intentionally - through presence, authenticity, or listening - to influence others without relying on authority or pressure?

Day 19: Building Circles That Elevate

"Surround yourself with only people who are going to lift you higher." ~ Oprah
Winfrey

Who we invite into our inner circles determines so much more than we realize
- our energy, our mindset, our emotional climate, and even the pace at which
we grow. We can feel the difference when we're around people who elevate
others compared to those who don't. Some people lift the atmosphere; others
quietly drain it. And for a long time, I held onto a relationship that taught me
exactly that.

I had a friend I kept close solely because of how long I had known them. Years
of shared memories made it feel like loyalty meant staying connected - even
when the relationship no longer aligned with who I was becoming. Over time,
this person grew increasingly hostile - about themselves, about others, about
life. Every conversation felt heavy. I found myself bracing for impact before
answering the phone, preparing for the next wave of criticism or self-doubt
I'd have to carry.

It became mentally exhausting. I loved this person, but loving them did not
mean sacrificing my own emotional health. One day, I realized something had
to change. I had to distance myself - not out of spite, not out of anger, but out
of self-respect. I needed to be intentional about the type of circle I wanted
to build: one filled with people who were positive, motivated, hopeful, and
reflective of the future I desired for myself.

75

Life brings enough challenges on its own. I wanted conversations that poured back into me, not ones that left me depleted.

When I created my small but mighty circle, everything shifted. These were people who spoke life, not limitations. People who encouraged growth, not gossip. They were leaders in their own lives - thoughtful, grounded, and committed to making an impact. And whenever I didn't feel my best, their belief in me held me up. I became extrinsically motivated when my internal motivation felt dim.

I would leave our conversations feeling lighter, clearer, and more aligned - because these relationships weren't transactional. They were transformational. We poured into one another with honesty and love. We held each other through wins and challenges. We still do.

And I take pride in that. In choosing well. In cultivating relationships that have real value - relationships built on accountability, support, trust, and genuine care. In these spaces, vulnerability wasn't a risk; it was welcomed. Sharing dreams wasn't met with jealousy; it was met with excitement.

Finding trustworthy individuals isn't always easy. But one thing I've learned is that creating an elevating circle begins with you. You must value yourself first. You must set the tone for the type of energy, integrity, and alignment you allow into your life. When you do, the right people begin to appear - not because of coincidence, but because your standard shifts.

And this isn't just personal - it's leadership.

We cannot lead effectively if we are surrounded by relationships that drain us, diminish us, or dull our vision. Leaders thrive in environments that challenge, uplift, and expand them. The right circle will elevate your mindset, confidence, creativity, and ability to drive meaningful impact.

When your relationships nourish you, your leadership becomes more authentic, grounded, compassionate, and strong. The people in your circle shape the leader you become - and the leader you are capable of being.

The right people in your circle won't just support you. They will help you rise.

Self-Reflection Questions

Which relationships in my life elevate me, and which ones drain me - and what boundaries or decisions do I need to make because of that?

How can I intentionally cultivate a circle that reflects the person and leader I am becoming, rather than the person I used to be?

Day 20: Legacy - What You Leave Behind

"If you have some power, then your job is to empower somebody else." ~ *Toni Morrison*

When most people think about leaving a legacy, they imagine the very end of life - what will be said about them, what will remain when they're gone. But true legacy is not something reserved for the final chapter. It is written in the small, intentional moments that make up our everyday lives.

Legacy is built in the micro-experiences:

How we show up.

How we listen.

How we support.

How we speak to others.

How we navigate challenges.

How we lead when no one is watching.

One question I consistently ask myself is, How do others experience me? That question alone has guided the way I want to show up for others - consistently, responsibly, and with intention. And I believe it's a question we all should consider. Because legacy is not about perfection or performance; it's about presence. It's about the imprint we leave on the hearts, minds, and spirits of the people we encounter.

When we think about legacy, many of the people who come to mind may be individuals we've never met. People like Maya Angelou - whose strength, vulnerability, and command of language have shaped generations. Her words have traveled through time and into our lives, reminding us that legacy is not limited by proximity. It's carried through influence, through impact, through truth.

I often bring her words to light because they encourage others to reflect, learn, grow, and rise. That, to me, is legacy in motion - ripples of wisdom that outlive the moments they were spoken in.

But legacy also shows up in the leaders we meet in our everyday lives. I've had leaders who forever changed my understanding of influence, not because of their position, but because of how they made people feel. They weren't loud; they were consistent. They weren't perfect; they were present.

They left a legacy through their daily interactions:

the time they took to develop others,

the care they showed in guiding teams,

The commitment they had to elevating people professionally and personally.

Their impact wasn't accidental - it was intentional. They poured into others, understanding that great leadership multiplies. And because of that, the people they supported went on to lead, inspire, and uplift others. That is legacy: not what you do alone, but what you empower others to do long after you're no longer in the room.

Legacy is ultimately about how people feel after experiencing us. Do they feel seen? Supported? Encouraged? Challenged in the right ways? Better because we crossed paths?

Not everyone will like you, agree with you, or understand you – that's not the goal. Legacy isn't about being liked. Legacy is about being responsible with your presence. It's about leading by example, especially when things get difficult, uncomfortable, or unseen.

Because someone is always watching.

A colleague.

A child.

A mentee.

A future leader.

Someone who will model what they see in you.

The question is: What are we giving them to model?

Legacy is the invisible curriculum we teach through our actions. It's the standard we leave behind. It's the example that continues in rooms we may never enter. And whether we realize it or not, we are building it every single day.

So the real work is not waiting for legacy to happen – it's choosing to create it now, through intention, character, and the impact we leave in every interaction.

Self-Reflection Questions

What impression or feeling do I consistently leave with the people I encounter – and how does that align with the legacy I want to build?

Who has shaped my understanding of legacy, and how can I carry forward their impact through my own leadership and daily actions?

III

Part III: Leading Outward

Leadership is ultimately expressed through impact. This section explores how your inner work and practiced growth extend beyond you – shaping relationships, cultures, and communities. When you lead from the inside out, your influence becomes authentic, sustainable, and deeply human.

Day 21: Lifting As You Climb

"The function of freedom is to free someone else." ~ Toni Morrison

The most admirable leaders are those who strive to achieve their goals and, while doing so, have others in mind. They understand that leadership is not a solo ascent but a collective climb. These leaders naturally give credit to those who helped them get there, encourage those with emerging potential, delegate to those who lead well, and intentionally identify the strengths of others so they can be positioned to use them. What I've noticed is that these kinds of leaders share a core characteristic: they are secure within themselves. Confident, grounded, and unbothered by someone else shining. They lift others as they climb because they recognize there is enough room at the top for more than one.

Secure leaders are not afraid of the spotlight shifting toward someone else. In fact, they welcome it. They want the best for other people – even if it means those people receive opportunities bigger than what anyone imagined. Their leadership is not threatened by talent; it is inspired by it. When someone on their team surpasses expectations or outgrows a role, they don't shrink back or compete – they celebrate, support, and sponsor.

I've experienced both ends of this spectrum. I've had leaders who embodied this spirit of service and sponsorship. They spoke up for people in rooms they weren't in - and even more boldly, in rooms they were in. They advocated for talent, recommended people for stretch assignments, and placed them in opportunities that stretched their self-belief. These leaders became cheerleaders on the sidelines of others' success, genuinely excited when their people won. Their confidence allowed them to recognize potential rather than feel threatened by it. Because of that, the people they led grew - and so did the leader.

But I've also experienced the opposite: insecure leaders who close doors for the very people they lead simply because those individuals intimidate them. Instead of nurturing talent, they silence it. They choose what feels like a more straightforward path - hiring someone they can control rather than someone who might elevate the work. They often prefer less competent individuals, not because it serves the organization well, but because it makes the leader feel more powerful. Unfortunately, these kinds of leaders miss the bigger picture: someone with the ability to innovate, transform systems, and elevate the team is an asset, not a threat.

Insecure leadership is rooted in fear - fear of being overshadowed, fear of being replaced, fear of being revealed. In that fear, they may hide the person with true potential while still leveraging their ideas and innovation. They quietly pull from that person's brilliance because it is undeniably good, but they will not lift the person behind it. This kind of leadership diminishes everyone, including the leader themselves.

Witnessing both sides has shaped my own leadership values. It is motivation never to be the leader who holds someone back out of insecurity or intimidation. Instead, it is a commitment to lead by serving - to put others' needs before your own when it comes to the work. To show people the way, to teach them to lead, and to support them as they rise. Leading others to elevate is not just a generous act; it is a legacy-building one.

Because the truth is this: your success as a leader is not measured by how high you climb alone, but by how many people you have brought with you along the journey. Title may grant authority, but service grants influence. And lifting others as you climb - not only strengthens them, it strengthens you.

Self-Reflection Questions

Who are three people you can intentionally lift, support, or sponsor as you continue your own leadership journey?

In what ways can you shift your daily actions to reflect a leadership style rooted in service rather than self-protection?

Day 22: Mentorship - Guiding and Being Guided

"If you want to lift yourself, lift up someone else." ~ *Booker T. Washington*

As a leader, when you have effectively led yourself, others will naturally take notice. Your consistency, character, and clarity become visible, and soon enough, people may ask you to be their mentor. In other cases, mentorship emerges organically through the work - when you lead a team, offer guidance, and help others improve based on your knowledge, skills, and abilities. Whether mentorship is requested or inherited, one truth remains: it is an investment of time, presence, and intention.

Most of us in leadership roles lead whole lives - balancing personal responsibilities, professional commitments, and our own continued development. That is why mentorship must be approached thoughtfully. To mentor well, you must be intentional and selective about how many people you commit to guiding. Quality mentorship requires capacity. When your plate is already full, taking on too many mentees dilutes the impact you can have. The question then becomes: How do you ensure that every touchpoint is meaningful, strategic, and worthy of the person seeking your guidance?

Effective mentorship doesn't thrive on casual check-ins or occasional conversations. It thrives on structure and purpose. There should be clear goals, aligned expectations, and an intentional rhythm that drives ongoing engagement. This helps both the mentor and mentee stay anchored to why the relationship exists in the first place. When done well, mentorship produces outcomes that are transformational rather than transactional. It shifts from "tell me what to do" to "help me become who I'm capable of being."

Mentorship is not limited to formal pairings or scheduled conversations. It happens in everyday moments when you pause to share wisdom, elevate some-one's perspective, or challenge them to step beyond what feels comfortable. A single insight, delivered at the right time, can unlock confidence, clarity, or courage. This is why mentors must show up with intention - because every interaction holds the potential to move someone forward.

But mentorship isn't one-directional. While guiding others, leaders must also develop the ability to be guided. Growth requires openness. Wisdom requires humility. And leadership requires the willingness to hear feedback - even when it's uncomfortable.

As a leader, being open to feedback is non-negotiable. Guidance can come from a direct leader who sees your strategic blind spots, a business partner who experiences the impact of your decisions, a direct report who feels the effect of your leadership style, or a peer who observes you in real time. Sometimes, the most powerful feedback comes from someone who doesn't hold positional authority over you but has firsthand experience with how you show up.

Actual development happens when you allow yourself to listen deeply - to hear not just what is said, but why it is said. When you become curious about how others experience you, you unlock the ability to evolve. You learn what habits you need to gain to rise to the next level - and what habits you need to release to avoid becoming stuck. Remaining teachable is the most underrated leadership competency. It protects you from stagnation, arrogance, and the repetition of mistakes.

Mentorship, then, is both an offering and a receiving. It is guiding while being guided. It is giving and receiving wisdom while remaining open to it. It is shaping others while allowing yourself to be shaped. The leaders who grow the furthest are those who embrace both sides of mentorship with gratitude and humility.

When you mentor well, you multiply your impact. When you allow mentorship to shape you, you elevate your potential. And when both happen together, you develop not just as a leader, but as a whole person committed to growth, service, and transformation.

Self-Reflection Questions

Who are the individuals you can intentionally mentor with structure, purpose, and the capacity to create transformational impact?

What feedback have you been avoiding – and how might embracing it open the door to your next level of leadership?

Day 23: Advocacy - Using Your Voice for Change

"If you are neutral in situations of injustice, you have chosen the side of the oppressor." ~ Desmond Tutu

Advocacy is one of the most powerful expressions of leadership. It is the moment you decide your voice will not remain silent when change is needed - whether for yourself, your team, or the future you're responsible for shaping. As you continue leading from the inside out, advocacy becomes not only something you do but something you embody.

Advocacy begins with courageous clarity - the willingness to speak up even when it feels uncomfortable or easier to look away. Leadership will place you in situations where silence seems safe, where the room is quiet, and where naming the truth may create tension. But advocacy has never lived in comfort. It grows in the moments when someone needs to rise and say, "This matters," "This is unfair," or "This needs to change."

I recall a time when I needed to speak up for someone on my team whose voice wasn't being heard and whose work wasn't being seen. They worked diligently all year, consistently delivering high-quality results. Yet when performance discussions came around, senior leaders said they had no visibility into this person's contributions. It wasn't that they didn't value the work - they didn't know it existed.

In that moment, I realized advocacy was not optional. It was my responsibility.

I made it a priority to schedule time with leaders individually. In those meetings, I presented the work my team had produced, the outcomes they drove, and the impact their efforts had on the organization. I told the whole story - one that deserved to be told. And when visibility increased, so did opportunity. Doors that were previously closed began to open. Recognition found its way to the right people - not because the work changed, but because the awareness did.

That experience taught me something profound: people can only acknowledge what they can see. Advocacy bridges that gap. It ensures that effort is not overlooked and that talent does not remain hidden. Sometimes leaders don't deny recognition intentionally - they don't have the visibility they need to make informed decisions. Advocacy becomes the spotlight that illuminates what was always there but previously unseen.

But advocacy is not just about speaking - it is about acting with intention. Influence is what transforms advocacy into impact. It means using your position, relationships, and credibility to open doors, shift conversations, and gain access. It means recommending someone's name in a room they are not in, challenging outdated norms, or presenting information others may not have considered.

Your advocacy holds weight not because of the volume of your words, but because of the intention behind them.

And advocacy must also be consistent. Consistency builds trust - the kind that tells your team, "Your work will not go unseen as long as I have a voice." True advocacy shows up in the everyday moments:

- When you correct misinformation about someone's performance.
- When you redirect credit where it belongs.

- When you highlight strengths that others overlook.
- When you make sure your team's contributions are visible to decision-makers.

Over time, your consistency becomes part of your leadership identity. People begin to trust that you will speak truthfully, act reasonably, and follow through - not only when it benefits you but when it benefits others.

Advocacy requires courage, empathy, and conviction. It challenges comfort, disrupts silence, and demands intentional action. And while using your voice may be uncomfortable at times, the outcome is worth it: people are seen, opportunities expand, and cultures shift.

You don't advocate because it's easy. You advocate because someone's growth depends on it. Someone's confidence depends on it. Someone's future depends on it.

And when you choose to use your voice for change, you don't just shape the environment - you transform the people within it.

Self-Reflection Questions

Where in your leadership journey is someone depending on your advocacy to gain the visibility, credit, or opportunity they deserve?

What consistent actions can you take to ensure your voice creates meaningful and lasting change for those you lead?

Day 24: Collaboration - The Power in Partnership

"If you want to go fast, go alone. If you want to go far, go together." ~ African Proverb

Collaboration is one of the most transformative forces in leadership. It is the moment when ideas meet, perspectives merge, and talents intertwine to create something none of us could have built alone. Collaboration elevates our thinking, sharpens our decisions, and expands our impact. It is not just a strategy - it is a mindset, a posture, and a powerful form of partnership.

Over the past decade, I have had the honor of working in the airline industry, surrounded by individuals with diverse backgrounds, work experiences, skills, and perspectives. That environment became one of the richest classrooms I've ever known. Each day offered the opportunity to learn from someone new, hear a different outlook, or expand my understanding simply by being in conversation with others. Collaboration became a pathway to growth - not just for projects, but for me as a leader.

Working on projects with others, making challenging decisions in a room full of strong voices, or ideating a new program or concept with a team - these experiences showed me just how powerful collective effort can be. Collaboration isn't just a meeting or a brainstorming session. It is the beautiful exchange of ideas that accelerates innovation. It is the blending of strengths that makes solutions stronger. It is the willingness to see beyond your own approach and value what others bring to the table.

There is something almost euphoric about watching collaboration unfold. You can feel the energy shift when a team begins connecting ideas, filling gaps, challenging assumptions, and building something together. You see talent rise to the surface. You witness individuals find their voice in new ways. You watch ideas sharpen, evolve, and grow stronger through discussion. Collaboration has a way of bringing out brilliance that might otherwise remain hidden.

I have always been a fan of collaboration because I know its value. The people around us carry expertise we don't have, experiences we've never lived, and insights we may never discover on our own. When we bring those perspectives together, we create a powerful force for improvement. Teams become smarter. Solutions become sharper. Work becomes richer. And results become more impactful.

As leaders, it is our responsibility to drive collaboration across our teams, workplaces, or businesses, not as a forced requirement, but as a culture - an expectation that partnership is more potent than isolation. Collaboration requires curiosity, humility, and openness. It means releasing the mindset that we must have all the answers and instead embracing the truth that the best answers often emerge when voices align.

Strong collaboration doesn't just happen on its own. It is cultivated through intentional actions:

- Creating environments where people feel safe to speak up and contribute
- Encouraging cross-functional discussions that break down silos
- Allowing teams to challenge ideas without challenging each other
- Celebrating collective wins rather than spotlighting individual achievements
- Making space for disagreements that sharpen the outcome

• Recognizing that every person at the table adds something valuable

The leaders who cultivate collaboration become catalysts for innovation. They know that partnership amplifies impact. They know that diverse perspectives create stronger outcomes. They know that when a team works together with trust and purpose, they can solve problems faster, make better decisions, and move with greater unity.

Collaboration is more than teamwork. It is the belief that we are better together. It is the understanding that partnership multiplies potential. It is the confidence that when we combine our strengths, our impact expands beyond what any one of us could achieve alone.

Whether you are building a business, leading a team, developing a program, or making decisions that shape the future, collaboration will always be the bridge between vision and execution. It is the space where ideas grow, people thrive, and transformation takes root.

Leaders who embrace collaboration unlock a level of excellence that is almost impossible to replicate alone. And when you lead with partnership at the center, you don't just build stronger results - you build stronger people.

Self-Reflection Questions

Who can you intentionally collaborate with to expand your perspective and strengthen your ideas or decisions?

What steps can you take to create a culture of partnership, openness, and shared problem-solving within your team or business?

Day 25: Seeing What's Possible for Others

"If you can't see it in someone else, you can't expect them to see it in themselves." ~
Dr. Maya Angelou

I absolutely love it when leaders see the potential in others - when they get ahead of what they believe is possible for someone and hold a vision that stretches beyond current roles, confidence, or circumstances. There is something profoundly human about being truly seen - not for who you are today alone, but for who you are becoming.

Visionary leadership is not about charisma or titles. It is about belief. It is the quiet, steady decision to look at someone and say, I see more in you than you see in yourself - and I'm willing to walk with you until you do.

Some of the most transformational leaders I've encountered weren't the loudest in the room or the ones with the most power. They were the ones who noticed me. They saw something in me before I had language for it. Before I had confidence in it. Before I even believed it was possible.

I am the leader I am today because someone lifted me when I couldn't lift myself.

I remember a moment that shifted the trajectory of my career. A leader sat me down and told me that she - and a Director - saw me operating two levels higher than the role I was currently in. At the time, I was doing my job well, but I wasn't imagining myself beyond it. I was focused on delivering, not necessarily expanding. Yet they saw something else: capability, readiness, and potential that hadn't yet been fully activated.

Instead of keeping that vision to themselves, they acted on it.

They placed me on high-visibility projects. They gave me exposure to leaders and conversations I hadn't previously had access to. They positioned me in spaces that stretched me while also supporting me. They didn't just tell me they believed in me - they designed opportunities that required me to step into that belief.

That exposure led to my next role - one that was perfectly aligned with my background, strengths, and natural way of leading. And in that role, I thrived. Not because I suddenly became someone new, but because I was finally in a space that allowed me to be fully myself. Most would agree it was an ideal position for me. What they didn't always see was that it started long before the title - with someone's vision.

That is the power of seeing what's possible for others.

Visionary leaders don't wait for people to check every box before they invest in them. They don't require perfection or complete confidence as a prerequisite for opportunity. Instead, they understand that belief often precedes performance. That people rise not only to expectations, but to environments that are intentionally designed to call forth their best.

When leaders lean into their people's strengths, everyone benefits. It's good for the individual, the leader, the business, and the organization as a whole. It creates momentum, engagement, and trust. It turns work into purpose and teams into communities.

But seeing potential doesn't mean ignoring growth areas.

As leaders, we must also be willing to stretch people - especially in what I like to call their areas of opportunity. Visionary leadership holds both grace and challenge. It says, I see your strengths - and I also see where you can grow. I won't shrink you to keep you comfortable, but I also won't push you without support.

Challenging someone to do what they thought they couldn't do is an act of belief. It requires patience, clarity, and intentional setup for success. Not throwing people into the deep end, but teaching them how to swim - while reminding them they were always capable of floating.

This kind of leadership requires inner work. It demands that we lead from abundance rather than fear, from belief rather than control. When we are secure in ourselves, we are more willing to elevate others. When we lead from the inside out, we stop competing with the people we lead and start investing in who they are becoming.

I've committed myself to being that kind of leader.

I choose to see the best in people - even when they can't see it yet. I decide to name strengths out loud, create space for growth, and hold vision with patience because I know firsthand how life-changing it can be when someone sees you clearly and refuses to let you stay small.

That is visionary leadership.

Not seeing what's possible for yourself alone - but seeing what's possible for others and helping them grow into it.

Self-Reflection Questions

Who in your life or career first saw your potential before you did - and how did that belief shape who you are today as a leader?

Who are you currently leading that may need borrowed belief from you, and what is one intentional way you can create space for them to thrive?

Day 26: Integrity - Doing What's Right When No One Is Watching

"Integrity is doing the right thing, even when no one is watching." ~ Dr. Martin Luther King Jr.

I believe integrity doesn't come in packages. You either have it or you don't. And while that may sound absolute, I also think something just as important: integrity can be chosen. If someone hasn't operated with integrity in the past, there is always the possibility of change, because integrity is not a personality trait. It's a decision. One that can be made at any point.

As leaders, we must be able to do right by ourselves and by others - not based on how we are perceived, not on who is watching, and not on what our supporters, peers, or critics think of us - but because we genuinely want to be good. Because it matters to us. Because it aligns with who we believe ourselves to be.

When integrity is genuine on the inside, it stops being a performance. It becomes a mindset, not a perceived behavior. And when integrity is internalized, we don't need an audience to guide our actions. We do what's right regardless of who is paying attention - because it's not about recognition, reputation, or reward.

It's about choices.

Integrity shows up in the choices we make when cutting corners would be easier, when silence would be more convenient, when no one would ever know if we chose differently. True integrity is consistently choosing the path of what's right - especially when there is no immediate benefit for doing so.

Always.

This is where many misunderstand integrity. They see it as a public-facing trait - something to be demonstrated when stakes are high, or eyes are watching. But integrity is actually built in the small, quiet moments. In the emails you don't have to send. The credit you give when you could have taken it. The truth you tell when a softer version would have protected you.

Over time, those choices accumulate.

And trust is the outcome.

Building trust with others is not something you can demand or manufacture. It is an output of integrity. People will know you're the real deal, not because you say the right things, but because you've consistently made the right choices. They may not always be able to name it, but they can feel it. Integrity leaves a residue.

This is where psychological safety begins.

Psychological safety exists when people believe they are led by someone they can trust - someone whose words and actions align, whose values don't shift based on convenience or pressure. In organizations, this kind of leadership creates cultures where people feel safe to speak up, to take risks, and to be honest. They know the ground beneath them is stable.

But integrity matters not only in companies.

As a business owner, integrity becomes the foundation of your brand - whether you intend it to or not. Your customers need to know they are being served honestly and with care. The people who work with or for you need to know they are being led with fairness and consistency. Integrity is what allows people to trust you with their time, money, ideas, and energy.

And trust, once broken, is costly to rebuild.

Leading with integrity requires inner discipline. It asks us to examine not just what we do, but why we do it. Are our decisions rooted in fear or in values? In image or in alignment? Integrity invites us to remain whole - to choose consistency between our inner beliefs and our outer actions.

This is what it means to lead from the inside out.

When integrity is a mindset rather than a performance, leadership becomes steady. Clear. Trustworthy. People don't have to wonder who you'll be depending on the room you're in. They know. And that knowing creates confidence, loyalty, and respect.

Integrity may not always be loud, but it is always powerful. And in the end, it is one of the few things that speaks for you - even when you are not in the room.

Self-Reflection Questions

When no one is watching, what values guide your decisions - and where might there be misalignment between what you believe and what you practice?

How does your level of integrity show up in the trust others place in you as a leader, business owner, or partner?

Day 27: Innovation - Leading with Courage and Creativity

"Don't be limited by other people's limited imaginations." ~ Dr. Mae Jemison

I am a creative. And the moment I can no longer create or innovate, I feel stagnant. When ideas are restricted, when curiosity is stifled, or when there is no room to challenge what already exists, something in me shuts down. I don't just enjoy innovation - I need it. It's how I stay engaged, energized, and connected to my work.

I thrive in environments where the status quo isn't treated as sacred, but as something to be examined. Where innovation is welcomed when it's necessary, and new ways of thinking are not dismissed simply because they are unfamiliar. There is something deeply fulfilling about bringing a new thought, idea, or concept to the table - and even more fulfilling when that idea is genuinely considered.

Because of this, I naturally lead in a way that creates room for others to do the same.

I allow those I lead to be open and free to express what they feel and how they believe things should be done. Not in a way that is chaotic or unstructured, but in a human way. I want people to feel they can contribute without pressure - without the fear of judgment, dismissal, or being labeled as "too much" or "off track."

Innovation cannot exist where fear lives.

While not every idea will be implemented – and while everything must ultimately be done within reason and supported by purpose – it is still important to gather all ideas. To leave no one behind. To make space for voices that may be quieter, unconventional, or still forming. Only then can leaders and teams collectively decide which direction to move in.

This is what inclusive innovation looks like.

One creative mind alone can spark an idea – but innovation is fully realized when creativity is unleashed, shared, and shaped together. A leader may be innovative, but that creativity does no good if it's hoarded or controlled. Innovation flourishes when leaders dare to loosen their grip and trust the collective.

And courage is required - on both sides.

It takes courage for someone to share an idea, especially in environments where being wrong has consequences or where difference has historically been discouraged. It also takes courage for a leader to truly listen - to resist the urge to dominate the direction, to embrace a variety of perspectives, and to lead with inclusivity rather than ego.

Leading with innovation means being willing to say, I don't have all the answers. It means choosing curiosity over control. It means understanding that the best ideas often emerge from collaboration, not hierarchy.

When innovation is present, engagement follows.

People are more interested in the work when they feel they have a voice in shaping it. They are more invested when they know their ideas matter. Innovation keeps teams energized, relevant, and willing to stay the course - even when the work is hard, or the path forward is unclear.

This is leadership from the inside out.

When leaders are secure enough to welcome creativity - both their own and others' - they create environments where people feel alive, valued, and inspired. Innovation then becomes more than a strategy; it becomes a culture. One rooted in courage, creativity, and collective ownership.

And in those environments, people don't just work.

They build.

Self-Reflection Questions

Where in your leadership or work have you felt most alive and creative - and what conditions made that possible?

How are you currently creating space for others to share ideas freely, and what might need to shift to foster more courageous innovation?

Day 28: Empowerment - Unlocking Potential in Others

"As you grow older, you will discover that you have two hands - one for helping yourself, the other for helping others." ~ Audre Lorde

I've discussed previously how important it is to lift as you climb. Empowerment is one of the most explicit expressions of that belief. When leaders empower people to reach their fullest potential, it benefits not only the individual but also the leader and the business. Empowerment multiplies impact. It creates momentum that no single person could sustain on their own.

But empowerment is often misunderstood.

It is not limited to observing talent and asking people to do what they are already good at - or what they could be better at. True empowerment goes deeper. It is entrusting people with responsibility and believing in them enough to allow them to carry out their work to the best of their ability. It is choosing trust over control.

And where empowerment exists, micromanagement cannot.

There is no room for micromanaging when the goal is to develop people. Micromanagement may feel productive in the short term, but it is a potent disruptor to growth. It communicates doubt rather than belief. It keeps people dependent instead of capable. And over time, it erodes confidence, creativity, and engagement.

To empower others, we must make space for them to thrive and grow - to think on their own and put their decision-making skills to work. Empowerment invites people into ownership. It says, I trust you to figure this out, and I'm here to support you, not hover over you.

I once had a micromanager, and that experience alone is enough to make someone want to run fast. I know I did. No matter how much you enjoy the work, being led by someone who constantly oversees, corrects, or controls every detail drains energy and motivation. Often, the person doing this may not even realize they're micromanaging - which is why self-awareness is essential in leadership.

Empowering leadership requires restraint. It asks leaders to examine their own need for control, certainty, or validation. It challenges us to ask: Am I leading to feel needed, or am I leading to develop others?

Being an empowering leader means allowing people to mess up when they need to - and helping them learn from it. It means being a teacher, not someone waiting for a mistake to say, I told you so. Growth doesn't happen through perfection; it occurs through experience, reflection, and guidance.

When leaders choose empowerment, they shift from being the hero of the story to being the guide. They focus less on proving their own competence and more on cultivating it in others. This kind of leadership requires humility. It requires patience. And it requires a long-term view.

Because empowerment is not about you.

It's about helping others become who they need to be.

When people are empowered, they show up differently. They take initiative. They think critically. They build confidence in themselves and in their abilities. And when they succeed, the entire organization moves forward - not because one person carried the load, but because leadership was shared.

This is leadership that lasts.

This is how potential is unlocked.

Self-Reflection Questions

Where in your leadership are you truly empowering others - and where might control or micromanagement be limiting growth?

How can you shift from doing or deciding for others to creating space for them to think, choose, and learn on their own?

Day 29: Balance - Sustaining Yourself While Leading

"We have to talk about liberating minds as well as liberating society." ~ Angela Davis

The phrase I often use is, "**We cannot pour from an empty cup.**" It's simple, but it's true. As leaders, sustaining ourselves is not optional - it requires intentional effort. Balance does not happen by accident, and it does not come after the work is done. It must be built into how we lead if we want to lead effectively over time.

Too many people I know have sacrificed their mental and physical health in the name of leadership. Working too much and taking on added stress, and saying yes when their capacity was already stretched thin. And often doing all of this without having any remedial plan in place to take care of themselves in the process. Somewhere along the way, the expectation became that leadership requires self-sacrifice at the expense of self-preservation.

But leadership should not cost you your health.

When leaders run on empty, it eventually shows. Decision-making becomes reactive. Patience wears thin. Creativity fades. Presence is replaced by survival mode. And while the work may still get done, the way it gets done begins to suffer.

Being present is key.

Presence requires energy. It requires clarity. It requires a leader who is not constantly pulled in a hundred directions, but who can show up fully - mentally, emotionally, and physically. Balance allows leaders to be present, not just available. There is a difference.

Sustaining yourself also means understanding that balance looks different in every season. There will be times when the work requires more of you, and other times when rest and restoration must take priority. Balance is not about equal time - it's about honest awareness. Knowing when to lean in and when to step back without guilt or justification.

This level of awareness requires leaders to listen to themselves. Your body will tell you when you are tired. Your mind will say to you when you are overloaded. Ignoring those signals doesn't make you strong - it makes burnout inevitable. Balance is the discipline of paying attention before exhaustion forces your hand.

Boundaries play a critical role here. Boundaries are not limitations; they are protections. They allow leaders to sustain their energy, focus, and effectiveness. When leaders fail to set boundaries, they don't just deplete themselves - they unintentionally teach others that overextension is the standard.

Whether we realize it or not, we model balance for those we lead.

When leaders glorify busyness, constant availability, and burnout, it becomes part of the culture. But when leaders prioritize rest, take breaks, and respect their own limits, they permit others to do the same. Balance, when practiced openly, creates healthier teams and more sustainable organizations.

Leading from the inside out means recognizing that your well-being directly impacts your leadership. You cannot lead others well if you are disconnected from yourself. Caring for your mental, emotional, and physical health is not selfish - it is responsible leadership.

Balance is not stepping away from leadership. It is what allows leadership to endure.

When leaders choose sustainability over constant sacrifice, they show that leadership can be powerful and humane. That success does not have to come at the cost of health. And that longevity, not burnout, is the goal.

Because in the end, we truly cannot pour from an empty cup.

Self-Reflection Questions

In what ways have you been pouring from an empty cup, and what has it been costing you?

What intentional boundary or practice can you put in place to help you lead with greater presence and sustainability in this season?

Day 30: Leading From the Inside Out - The Journey Continues

"We are always in the process of becoming." ~ bell hooks

Leading from the inside out is not a destination. It is not a box you check, a skill you master, or a moment you arrive at and stay. It is a **lifelong journey** - one that evolves as you evolve, and deepens as you become more honest with yourself.

What I've come to understand is this: the inner work never ends. And that's not a weakness of leadership - it's the strength of it.

Each chapter of this book speaks to a different expression of leadership - vision, integrity, innovation, empowerment, balance - but they all come back to the same truth: **who you are on the inside shapes how you lead on the outside**. As your life changes, as your responsibilities grow, and as new challenges arise, leadership will continue to ask something new of you.

Leading from the inside out requires ongoing self-reflection. It asks you to pause and examine your intentions, your patterns, and your growth edges. It invites you to revisit your values - not once, but often - to ensure your leadership remains aligned with who you are becoming.

Because leadership is not static.

113

What worked in one season may no longer serve you in the next. The leader you were five years ago may not be the leader your current environment requires. Leading from the inside out means having the courage to evolve - to release old versions of yourself without judgment and step into new ones with humility.

This kind of leadership is not about perfection. It is about **consistency**. Choosing alignment again and again. Choosing integrity even when it's uncomfortable. Choosing curiosity when certainty feels safer. Choosing to empower others rather than control outcomes and choosing balance so you can keep showing up whole.

And sometimes, choosing to begin again.

There will be moments when you get it wrong. Moments when fear leads instead of faith. Moments when exhaustion clouds judgment or old habits resurface. Leading from the inside out does not mean avoiding these moments - it means taking responsibility for them, learning from them, and allowing them to refine you.

The journey continues because leadership is lived in real time.

And the impact of this kind of leadership often reaches farther than you'll ever see. When you do the inner work, it ripples outward - into teams, organizations, families, and communities. It shows up in the leaders you develop, the cultures you shape, and the people who feel seen, supported, and strengthened because of your leadership.

You may never fully know the lives you influence simply by choosing to lead with self-awareness, courage, and care. But the ripple exists nonetheless.

Leading from the inside out is a commitment to keep becoming - so your leadership can keep serving. It is the understanding that the work within you is never wasted — every moment of reflection, every complicated conversation with yourself, every intentional choice compounds over time.

And so, the journey does not end here.

It continues every day you choose to lead with intention.

Every day you choose alignment over approval.

Every day you choose to grow - so others can grow too.

<u>Self-Reflection Questions</u>

As you reflect on your leadership journey so far, what inner work is being invited of you in this current season?

How will you intentionally continue leading from the inside out - long after this chapter ends?

Conclusion

Closing: Carrying the Work Forward

This book was never meant to give you a checklist for leadership. It was meant to invite you into a **practice** - one that begins within you and expands outward into every space you occupy.

You started with the inner foundations: vision, values, confidence, resilience, energy, and courage. These chapters asked you to look inward first, because leadership that lasts is built from the inside out. Before you can lead others with clarity, you must know what anchors you. Before you can move boldly, you must understand what steadies you.

From there, you moved into the daily work - the practices that shape how you show up over time. Discipline. Boundaries. Emotional intelligence. Authenticity. Purpose. Gratitude. Adaptability. Influence. Relationships. Legacy. These are not one-time decisions; they are choices we make again and again. This is where leadership becomes real - where intention meets consistency.

And finally, you stepped into leading outward.

Service. Mentorship. Advocacy. Collaboration. Visionary leadership. Integrity. Innovation. Empowerment. Balance. These chapters reflect leadership beyond self-leadership that multiplies impact, lifts others, and creates environments where people can thrive. This is leadership that understands its responsibility and honors its reach.

But here's the truth: **none of this is linear**.

You will revisit these chapters in different seasons of your life. Some will feel like reminders. Others will feel like invitations. There will be moments when you are strong in one area and stretched in another. That does not mean you are failing - it means you are growing.

Leading from the inside out is not about getting it right all the time. It's about staying honest, staying aware, and staying committed to becoming. It's about alignment over approval, courage over comfort, and sustainability over performance.

As you close this book, the work does not end - it continues with you.

In the conversations you choose to have. In the boundaries you decide to honor. In the way you treat people when no one is watching. In how you care for yourself while carrying responsibility. In how you lift others as you rise.

Leadership is not just what you do - it is who you are becoming.

And if you continue to lead from the inside out, your impact will extend far beyond what you can see. Into people. Into culture. Into legacy.

This is the journey.

And it continues - with you.

Also by Diara Kendrich

Diara Kendrich's books equip individuals, professionals, and leaders with practical tools to lead themselves well, show up with intention, and navigate workplace dynamics with confidence, clarity, and compassion - at every stage of their career.

Put A Down Payment On Your Career
A practical and empowering guide for professionals ready to stop waiting for permission and start investing - intentionally and strategically - in their own growth, influence, and future.

Your Customer Service Selfie
A fresh perspective on customer experience that challenges individuals to examine how attitudes, behaviors, and everyday interactions shape trust, loyalty, and brand reputation.

Who Farted in the Boardroom?
A candid and engaging take on workplace conflict that helps leaders address tension, navigate tough conversations, and restore alignment - without blame, avoidance, or unnecessary drama.

www.ingramcontent.com/pod-product-compliance
Lightning Source LLC
Chambersburg PA
CBHW010936120626
46554CB00007B/2492